IMAGES
of Scotland

BATHGATE

IMAGES
of Scotland

BATHGATE

William F. Hendrie

TEMPUS

First published 2001
Copyright © William F. Hendrie, 2001

Tempus Publishing Limited
The Mill, Brimscombe Port,
Stroud, Gloucestershire, GL5 2QG
www.tempus-publishing.com

ISBN 0 7524 2125 5

Typesetting and origination by
Tempus Publishing Limited
Printed in Great Britain by
Midway Colour Print, Wiltshire

Jarvey Street, Bathgate.

Jarvey Street provides one of the last remaining links with Bathgate's old town.

Contents

Acknowledgements

My thanks to Dr Arthur Down for taking many of the modern photographs which contrast so graphically with the archive ones supplied by West Lothian Council Library. My thanks also to Mrs Dorothy Cook for providing additional photographs from the collection belonging to her late mother, Mrs Robina Walker and to the head teachers of local schools for other pictures. I am especially grateful to West Lothian Local Studies Librarian Sybil Cavanagh for her patience and co-operation during my researches at library headquarters at Connelly House and to Guthrie Pollock and my publisher Campbell McCutcheon for their help with the layout of this book. The postal information was provided by William Cochrane.

Overlooking the grounds of Kaim Park Hotel, this old Bathgate farm steading has been painstakingly restored and now forms a very attractive cluster of houses.

Introduction

Bathgate is situated approximately midway between Edinburgh and Glasgow on the busy M8 motorway that links the two cities. It is therefore a town passed by many, but visited by few. This is a pity, for it is a West Lothian town with much to offer visitors and residents alike. Its delights range from the facilities of its beautiful Peace Park, with the longest indoor running track in Britain, to its Bennie Museum, which boasts one of the most interesting local collections in the country. As a modern industrial town it comes as a surprise to discover what a rich and varied history Bathgate has, including being the site of the world's first commercial oil refinery and the birth place of Sir James Young Simpson, the royal surgeon who pioneered the use of anaesthetics in surgery.

Bathgate's earliest link with the past, its castle, is now only a proud symbol on the burgh's coat of arms. In the thirteenth and fourteenth centuries, though, it was one of the most important keeps in Scotland, often visited by the royal family and their courtiers while on hunting expeditions from Linlithgow Palace. It may indeed have been the 'House in the Midst of the Boar Wood', from which Bathgate is said to derive its name. Built on the south side of the town on what is now the golf course, the castle was the home of Princess Marjory, daughter of King Robert the Bruce of Bannockburn fame. Her father included it as part of her rich wedding dowry when she married Walter the Lord High Steward of Scotland, thus founding the royal house of Stewart. Marjory and Walter are remembered on the first Saturday of June each year when they are the principal characters portrayed by local school children at the town's annual Newland's Day Procession.

Newland's Day is another proud reminder of Bathgate's colourful past. It is named after John Newland, the local 'lad o' pairts' who in the eighteenth century braved the rigours of the Atlantic Ocean to sail to the West Indies, where he made his fortune as a plantation owner in Jamaica. He never returned to his hometown, but clearly he never forgot it either as, when he died in 1799, he left the whole of his estate to found a secondary school to provide free education for the 'bairns of Bathgate'. Unfortunately for the town, Newland's relatives contested the will, but in the end the townsfolk led by their Provost, John Marjoribanks of Balbardie House, won their case at the Court of Session. Although the funds which they were granted were reduced, the new Bathgate Academy was built. This fine neo-classical building with its pillared facade still dominates the hillside above the town. It is from its steps that one of the school's many distinguished former pupils is honoured each June with an invitation to deliver the annual Newland's Oration. For many years its premises have been part of the adjoining West Lothian College of Further

Education, while Bathgate's secondary age pupils are now educated in the modern premises of the new academy on the eastern outskirts of the town and at St Kentigern's Academy in neighbouring Blackburn. (Now that West Lothian College has moved to Livingston a new use is being sought for the old academic building.)

It was at Blackburn also that Bathgate's largest modern industry, the huge British Leyland Truck and Tractor Works, was built during the 1960s. Sadly, like the town's traditional industries of coal and textiles, this works is now a thing of the past and the town has struggled in recent years to find employment for its population. Now this is changing. The establishment of modern computer-based factories, together with the town's restored passenger railway link with Edinburgh, have made the town an attractive place for young families to make their homes and the fortunes of Bathgate have been revived.

This book is designed to provide long-time residents and newcomers alike with a great deal of background information and pictures both old and modern of a place that they are proud to call their home.

One

The Heart of Bathgate

For over a century George Square has been Bathgate's busy town centre – where George Street, North Bridge Street, Whitburn Road and King Street all converge. Many older residents still refer to this popular meeting place by its traditional name of the Steel Yard. This is a title derived, however, not from Bathgate's well-known connections with the heavy metal industries through the famous North British Steel Factory and other local works, but from the town's former links with the textile industry. For George Square took its original name from a yard-long length of metal embedded in the surface of the roadway, against which the local weavers used to check their measures to ensure the cloth which they produced was of the correct width and length. A similar metal measuring rod can be seen displayed on the wall of the Ell Shop in the Perthshire town of Dunkeld, but Bathgate's original yard of steel has long since disappeared. The area named after it yet remains a focal point for local inhabitants, many of whom have memories of it over the years from shopping at Greig's Department Store, to meeting there on first dates before going on to the pictures at Green's Pavilion and the Regal Cinema. The town's main post office was for many decades situated here, as was its best hotel, the Royal, which originally had a bustling coach yard and stables situated behind it with horses and carriages for hire. In contrast to the clatter of horses' hooves and the noise of the engines of the cars and buses revving up in years gone by, George Square is now a pedestrian precinct, as is adjoining George Street. George Street too has seen a change of name: formerly it was Engine Street, after the steam engine once situated at its top near its junction with North Bridge Street. This device was used to pump water form the workings of the coal pits that ran under the town. During the 1930s, however, it was apparently decided that the most important shops and businesses in Bathgate, the majority of which congregated along this street, deserved a more distinguished address. Thus Engine Street was renamed George Street after the reigning King George V; the Steel Yard was also re-christened at this time.

As the town's meeting place, it was fitting that George Place and George Street, seen running off it to the right, were chosen as the centrepiece for this local postcard printed in the 1930s. The single car travelling along South Bridge Street and the few motor vehicles parked along the right hand side of George Street make the area look pedestrianized. This change did not in reality take place until many decades later, by which time the increase in traffic had also necessitated the installation of traffic lights at the junction with Whitburn Road. The publishers of this postcard make Bathgate appear a rural retreat with their choice of Torphichen Parish Church and Preceptory, the River Avon near Wallace's Cave and the Rock Garden in Kirkton Park as the other views on this composite card. In truth, by the years immediately preceding the Second World War, Bathgate was an important industrial centre, with Hopetoun Street as its other shopping area. This street is depicted in the fourth photograph on this card. It is interesting to note the linen awnings fronting the shops not to provide cover for shoppers in inclement weather, but to protect goods displayed in their windows from the rays of the sun.

This very early postcard of Engine Street gives a glimpse of the original St David's Church, whose small turreted belfry rises above the clump of trees. It was demolished in 1905 and replaced the following year with the present church, the impressive Venetian-style tower of which dominates the scene in the central picture on the previous postcard of the town.

The present St David's Church had still not been built when this early postcard view was taken, capturing for posterity the local laddies playing in the middle of George Street. They were enjoying their game in front of the tree-lined garden of the home of the local doctor, whose waiting room and surgery was lit at night by the gas lamp on the extreme left of the photo. The GP's house was later demolished to make way for the building of more shops.

The gentleman's Parisian-style urinal was still a curiously prominent feature of the Steel Yard several years later after the construction of the new St David's Church, when this other postcard view was taken from about the same spot looking north along the length of Engine Street.

This view across the almost deserted Steel Yard to South Bridge Street on the left and Engine Street on the right was also taken prior to 1906 and the erection of the new St David's Church. Of interest in the foreground is the Parisian-style gentleman's public convenience. Built of iron, it can be seen standing in front of the premises of the Royal Hotel, which is seen in more detail in a later photograph.

This early motor bus operated the public service from Bathgate to West Calder. It was owned by the S.M.T., the Scottish Motor Traction Co., the largest bus operator in the area from which present operator First Bus can trace its origins. The S.M.T. had its headquarters in Edinburgh, as noted above the company's crest painted on the door of the vehicle. The company's local depot was in Whitburn Road where the bus station was also situated. The well-known S.M.T. drivers Mick Coyle and Jack Dyer are pictured in their navy blue uniforms, navy peaked caps and tall knee-length leather boots standing in front of the bus. On this occasion Mr Dyer was working as the bus conductor. The leather pouch in which he collected the fares and the metal punch with which he clipped the cardboard tickets he issued can be seen slung over his shoulders. The ride from Bathgate to the Calders must have been a bumpy one, as the bus had hard rubber tyres. Its small carbide lamp headlights can also be seen

Unlike in the picture opposite, the tall tower of the new St David's Church was a well-established local landmark by the time this postcard view was published in the early 1920s. The unusual twin spires of Bathgate's Catholic Church in Livery Street can also be seen beyond the north end of Engine Street. A local public transport service had been started by this time and passengers can be seen waiting to board the motorised bus on the left side of the Steel Yard, from where it was about to depart for Torphichen and Linlithgow.

The name Engine Street appears on this early 1900s picture postcard view, taken and published after the completion of St David's Church's new premises in 1906. The men are standing outside the post office. After the post office moved to its current location on North Bridge Street, its former premises became the Royal Bank. The shop on the corner, described above the door as a dairy, sold a wider range of groceries than simply milk, butter and cheese, as the crowded displays in its windows show.

Steel Yard, Bathgate.

The linen awning is out over the window of the dairy in this picture postcard view, looking east along King Street. Notice the bus stopped opposite where the railway station is now situated and the second bus standing outside the former premises of the post office, from where the service to Edinburgh used to depart.

The Royal Hotel had bay windows on both the ground and first floors and a balustraded facade. Over the top bay window the word "Posting" is a reminder that until the coming of the railway in Victorian times the hotel was a regular stopping place for the stagecoaches which daily carried passengers between Edinburgh and Glasgow. The journey between the two cities was a long, slow and bumpy one; the stagecoaches took twelve wearisome hours to travel over roads which were muddy quagmires in winter and rutted dust bowls in summer. No matter what the season passengers must have welcomed the halt at Bathgate's Royal Hotel. Here the horses were either changed or fed and watered – an opportunity for passengers to enjoy a drink or hurriedly purchase some food to sustain them on the remainder of their journeys. The coaching yard was situated behind the hotel with an entrance from Engine Street. Mr W. White, the owner of the hotel whose name appears on the facade of the building, also made much of his profit from hiring out horses and a variety of different vehicles, from traps to landaus.

Two

Around The Burgh

Bathgate was created a Burgh of Barony by King Charles II in 1661, the year following his restoration to the throne after Britain's period as a republic under the rule of the Lord High Protector, Oliver Cromwell. Over a century and a half later in 1824, an Act of Parliament declared it a free and independent Burgh of Barony under the government of a Provost, three Bailies, twelve Councillors, a treasurer, a town clerk and a procurator fiscal. It remained an independent burgh until 1975, when the reform of local government masterminded by Lord Wheatley robbed it of its proud status. From then until 1996 it was administered as part of West Lothian District and became the district council's headquarters. Since 1997 it has been part of West Lothian Unitary Authority. An account of West Lothian published shortly after the end of the First World War in 1918 describes Bathgate as:

> *...a market town and police burgh whose industries include foundries, spade and shovel works and a distillery. It is railway junction of some importance and is the centre of a busy mining district of rapidly growing importance. Bridgend is a western suburb and Durhamtoun and Woodend are colliery villages in Bathgate Parish. The origin of the name is obscure, the earliest spellings being, Bathchet, Bathket and Barket.*

Other books have suggested the name may be derived either from 'the house in the boar wood' or from the Celtic for an 'enclosed sheep fold'. By 1900 the town covered an area in excess of 10,000 acres and by 1921 its population had grown to 8,226. It is now double that figure and, with many new homes under construction, is predicted to reach 19,000 by 2005.

Bathgate's coat of arms shows a heraldic depiction of the town's former castle, which was given as a dowry by King Robert the Bruce to his daughter Princess Marjory upon the occasion of her marriage in 1306 to Walter the Lord High Steward of Scotland. They made the castle their main residence and Walter lived there until his death in 1328. The Latin motto around the coat of arms may be translated as meaning 'For the common good'.

Bathgate lies in the lea of the Bathgate Hills, which rise to a height of 1,000ft behind the town. The hills are seen at the top of this early aerial photograph of the town, with Hopetoun Street and North Bridge Street slanting diagonally across the picture. One of the highest hills, the Knock, whose name simply means the Hill, belongs to the people of Bathgate. Other visible landmarks include the spire of the High Church to the left of North Bridge Street and the deep red sandstone tower of St David's Church to the right on George Street. The Steel Yard, or George Square as it is now, can be identified on the right hand lower edge of the picture and South Bridge Street curves from it to the left.

This attractive view appears, like the previous picture, to have been taken from the air, but it was in fact photographed from the tower of St David's Church. Looking to the north over George Street it shows the spire of the High Church standing out clearly in front of the sweeping outline of the Bathgate Hills. Amongst the shops on the east side of George Street can be seen the premises of John Hardy, a well-known draper whose firm traded in town for over a century.

This second photograph taken from the tower of St David's Church looks north east and encompasses Hopefield Lane, Bloomfield Place, Violet Bank and the graceful stone spire of St John's Church and its minister's manse in Mid Street. Behind it is the neo-classical facade of the original Bathgate Academy on the north side of Marjoribanks Street. This street was named appropriately after the town's former Provost who fought the court case to ensure the building of the school.

Postmarked 1908, this fine picture postcard view shows a horse-drawn delivery cart plodding its way along Mid Street as seen looking east from Hopetoun Street. The terraced houses on either side of the street are built of sandstone with slate roofs. The numerous chimney-stacks are a reminder of what a smoky old place Bathgate was when all of its houses were heated by open coal fires. The photograph appears to have been taken when many grown ups and children were making their way to or from work and school.

The same gas street lamp as in the previous photograph also features in this slightly later postcard of Mid Street taken in 1911 as part of Davidson's Real Photographic Series. It is interesting to recall that the town produced all of its domestic gas supply by the burning of coal at the local gas works. Mid Street is much quieter in this picture than it is nowadays. As in the previous picture there is a horse-drawn cart coming towards the photographer, who took this photo looking east from Hopetoun Street, but this time there is also a cart travelling away from him in the opposite direction.

In 1923 this is how Hopetoun Street looked from its junction with Marjoribanks Street. This postcard view was published as part of the Caledonian Series.

Looking in the opposite direction to the north this is how Hopetoun Street appeared ten years earlier in 1913 when it was photographed as part of the Davidson's Real Photographic series of postcards. Engine Street is seen branching to the right.

This picture postcard view again shows the junction of Hopetoun Street, George Street and North Bridge Street.

At one time this junction was the site of the fountain given to Bathgate to mark the completion and official opening of the local water works at Piershill. The fountain was later moved to what was considered by the local council to be a more appropriate site in the Steel Yard, but local people did not approve and nicknamed the junction of Hopetoun Street, North Bridge Street and George Street 'The Fountainless Cross'.

On warm days the controversial fountain was always a popular place to gather in the sunshine, as these lads did one long forgotten summer. After it was moved to George Square, the fountain was hidden from public view for many years, as during one of the many renovations of that area it was dismantled and stored away in the Burgh Yard.

Fortunately the founder and curator of the Bennie Museum, former Bathgate Academy art master and assistant headmaster of Murrayfield Primary School, Willie Millan, heard that the old fountain was still in existence and managed to find all of the pieces which he then painstakingly cleaned and restored. Now the fountain has once again been erected in the pedestrianized George Square, where it provides an attractive decorative feature and a link with Bathgate's past.

Another Bathgate landmark that has been given a new lease of life is the Art Deco-style Regal Cinema, which following its closure as a picture house was renovated and turned into a community theatre. The marquee over the entrance on which the latest films were advertised has been carefully preserved, as have the decorative glass panels that are a feature of the interior.

North and South Bridge Streets, Bathgate.

This postcard shows the same part of the town as it looked almost a century ago. The photograph on this card, postmarked 1912, was taken from the foot of Millburn Road looking towards the junction of North and South Bridge Streets.

Newspaper billboards relay the latest headlines outside Power's Newsagents Shop in South Bridge Street. The long, low, whitewashed, slate-roofed, single-storeyed building was later demolished and replaced by a two-storeyed one, which became well known as the premises of bookshop owner Bodo Jowet. During the 1960s, he established a flourishing business supplying all of West Lothian Education Authority's schools.

Another of Bathgate's early newsagents was in Engine Street at the corner of Engine Lane where the pumping engine which gave rise to these place names was situated. It is interesting to note that in these days, long before television or even radio news bulletins, the Airdrie Advertiser was circulated weekly in West Lothian. It found business sufficiently profitable to maintain an office in Bathgate above the newsagent from where its local reporter diligently wrote up and filed his copy by the deadline for each issue. The red pantile roofed newspaper office and the newsagent's shop below were demolished many decades ago, but interestingly newspapers and magazines are still sold from this site in George Street as it is now occupied by a branch of R.S. McColls. The fountain on the pavement kerb against which two of the boys in the picture are leaning is a reminder that many Bathgate homes did not have a running water supply and that water had to be collected in buckets and pails from these stand pipes in the street. Andrew Laing's clothiers shop is also a reminder of how life in Bathgate has changed over the years. There was far more scope for a small business like this in the town before car ownership encouraged local families to journey to larger shopping centres in neighbouring towns for their new suits and other outfitting requirements. Nowadays, cut-price discount outlets such as Freeport near West Calder and MacArthur Glen in Livingston make it even more difficult for local shops to compete.

A horse-drawn delivery cart is seen halted outside one of the shops in North Bridge Street, looking up the hill towards Hopetoun Street, in this picture postcard photograph. In front of the first awning a boy is walking along carrying a bundle on his head. On the opposite side of the street a red and white painted barber's pole juts out over the pavement.

This postcard of Hopetoun Street captured a moment of high drama in Bathgate in 1923, when subsidence caused by the collapse of underground coal pit workings resulted in local householders having to be hurriedly evacuated. Adding to the haste of the emergency evacuation was the fracture of a gas main resulting from this collapse, which led to fears of an imminent explosion. As the large crowd held back by two uniformed officers of the local police constabulary looked on, James Carlaw hastily stacked his furniture and other household possessions onto the back of an open lorry. Fortunately there was no further damage and Mr Carlaw and his neighbours were able to return to their homes. Half a century later, during the early 1970s, further subsidence below this part of the town, which is honeycombed with old coal pit workings, forced the demolition of several buildings and later Bathgate's new public library was also affected.

Bathgate Police were also to the fore in North Bridge Street when, during the First World War, this field ambulance was presented to the Red Cross. The presentation took place in front of D.R. Gordon's well-known ironmonger's store. The gentleman with the black bowler hat seated behind the wheel of the ambulance is the Rev. John Lindsay, minister of St John's Church, after whom, as chairman of the West Lothian Education Committee, the Lindsay High School was to be named. The name Linlithgowshire painted below the windscreen is a reminder that this was the original name for the county. All road vehicles registered in Linlithgowshire bore the letters SX as a prefix to their number, that on the ambulance thus reading SX 453.

Many Bathgate men sacrificed their lives in the trenches during the terrible years of the First World War and all of their names were recorded on the war memorial erected originally on the high ground overlooking the town. The names of local service personnel who died during the Second World War were also later recorded on tablets at the foot of the stone obelisk.

During the 1990s it was decided to move the war memorial from its rather remote hilltop site, which was proving difficult for older inhabitants to reach. A more convenient central site in Mid Street adjacent to St John's Church was chosen. This move was made possible through the involvement of popular television personality Anneka Rice of Channel Four's *Treasure Hunt* fame, who featured the tremendous amount of work and organisation involved in the move in another of her programmes, *Challenge Anneka*. The move to Mid Street met with general approval. The attractively maintained site is now also home to the plaque paid for and erected by pupils at Bathgate schools to show their sympathy for the boys and girls who were killed during the Dunblane School Massacre on March 13 1996. The plaque and the tree that they also planted as a tribute to the young lives lost in this tragic incident are shown on the left of the picture.

The grounds of Bathgate's historic Kirkton Church contain the grave of the town's Covenanting hero, James Davie. He was slain because of his religious beliefs by government dragoons during a running skirmish following a prayer meeting at Blackdub, near where Armadale Railway Station was later situated. Despite his massacre, many Bathgate people remained defiantly determined to worship in their own fashion. Driven from their churches, they held open-air services called 'conventicles' in the Bathgate Hills, with lookouts posted while worship took place. Communion vessels were even cleverly constructed so that bowls, stems and basins could all be swiftly hidden under jerseys, jackets and skirts if the red coats of the soldiers were spotted on the horizon. The lookouts would give early warning by imitating birdcalls, like the curlew's cry. On one occasion, however, the Bathgate Covenantors were rounded up by government troops to prevent them joining up with other supporters of the cause at Bothwell Bridge. Under the orders of Claverhouse they were marched twenty miles to Edinburgh where, as the city's jails were already filled to capacity, they were lodged for the night in the open air amongst the tombstones of Greyfriars Churchyard. During the days which followed, several of the Bathgate men were singled out and flogged with the cat-o'-nine-tails as a deterrent to the others. In the end they were all allowed to return home where they proudly continued to worship in the Protestant manner.

Bathgate bairns have always taken great pride in their town, but the impressive Scottish Baronial-style turreted Municipal Building depicted on this picture postcard never got beyond the planning stage. Even at the start of the 1900s, there were pressures on local government finance and Provost Robertson was thus never able to turn his dream into reality.

Armadale Road looking to the west, was the subject of this picture postcard. The view was taken from Bridgend and shows many interesting features pertaining to life in Bathgate prior to the outbreak of the First World War. These include the unmetalled surface of the road, the styles of dress of the local children and the gentleman on the right and the advertisements for both Cadbury's and Rowntree's chocolate displayed on the gable wall of the three-storeyed tenement building. As well as its many crowded homes, this building included a corner shop to meet the needs of the large families who inhabited them. In comparison to the houses in the tenement block, the cottages opposite with their own wrought-iron railing enclosed front gardens would have been expensive and were probably owned privately rather than rented.

On the outskirts of the town, Bathville Road had a distinctly rural look about it when it was photographed prior to the First World War for use on this pretty picture postcard. The inclusion of the lady and the two children standing on the pavement in the foreground adds to the interest, with the little girl wearing a white pinafore over her dress and the little boy a navy sailor suit and white sailor hat.

The style of dress of Bathgate bairns almost a century ago is further illustrated by this photograph, taken on the corner of Glasgow Road and Muir Road. The boys wear knickerbockers tucked in tightly at the knee and thick dark coloured woollen stockings, which were probably hand-knitted by their mothers. The caps that they are wearing may have been school caps. This suggests that the children may have been on their way to or from school when photographed here, leaning against the brick wall and wrought iron railings of the slate-roofed cottage.

If the boys and girls in the previous picture were coming to or from school, their route may well have taken them along Torphichen Street as shown in this picture postcard view, postmarked 1914. Bathgate Public School, or the Big Public as it was often known, had been opened ten years earlier in 1904 and catered for both primary and secondary pupils up to the age of fourteen after which they left to find work.

Torphichen Street led on out to Ballencrieff Toll where all vehicles, such as this pony and trap, had to halt at the little cottage on the left to pay a toll for the use of the road. This scene was photographed in 1903 for the R. and F. Local Views Series.

Ballencrieff Toll House is seen again in this picture taken five years later in 1908. It was part of the Milton Gazette Series and was numbered 3,620. The reason so many picture postcards were published often showing similar local views was the great demand for them as the easiest way to correspond in the days before many homes had telephones. A card posted first thing in the morning might well carry the message that the sender intended to pay a visit that same evening. The provision of an afternoon postal delivery would have ensured that it reached its destination in time. Postcards were inexpensive and rather than a plain white one, most people preferred to send one bearing a picture of a local beauty spot, such as the one captured here.

This is how Ballencrieff Toll on the busy main road between Bathgate and Torphichen now looks – fortunately passing vehicles no longer have to stop to pay a toll!

Three

Torphichen: The Old Village

The road from Ballencrieff Toll leads on to the village of Torphichen two miles further north. Torphichen came into existence before Bathgate as the lands around the village were given by King David I to the Knights of the Order of St John of Jerusalem, who built their Scottish headquarters there around the year 1165. The Preceptory, as it was named after the eight Christian precepts, proved so central that it was used to collect the ground rents due from the knights' Scottish properties including estates as near as Knightsridge in Livingston and as far away as Elgin. By the early 1200s, the knights shared their chapel with the local villagers as their parish church and this arrangement continued until the Reformation in 1560. At this time Sandilands, the Grand Master of the Order of St John, surrendered the knights' properties to the crown and in return received back Torphichen and other property in West Lothian as a personal secular grant to him. Possibly because of the wrath of the local people he chose not to return to Torphichen, but instead built a new home for himself and his family fifteen miles to the south in Mid Calder, where the present Lord Torphichen still lives. In his absence from the village, stones were plundered from the Preceptory for use in building local homes including Cathlaw House.

The Preceptory was in a ruinous condition when another of the area's lairds, Henry Gillon of Wallhouse, agreed in 1750 to pay for a new church to be built on the site of the old nave. The plans that he approved for this typically Presbyterian eighteenth-century place of worship included a laird's loft. He even gave an extra sum of money to include a fireplace so that if the minister's sermon went on too long he could keep himself warm. However, Gillon's plans to occupy the laird's loft were in for a shock. On the first Sunday that the church was completed in 1756, the absentee landowner Lord Torphichen rode up in his coach and announced that it was his right to sit there. Both men were lawyers in Edinburgh and so they resorted to the Court of Session to fight their dispute. After seven costly years of legal wrangling, the court decided in favour of Lord Torphichen. To this day it is his coat of arms which graces the balcony of the laird's loft, while those of the Gillon family are painted on one of the other galleries which they had to accept as second best. Nowadays the little parish church also contains the stalls of the Knights of St John, who still return once a year with drawn swords and banners flying to the site of their old headquarters (their modern headquarters are at St John's House in St John's Street off the Cannongate in Edinburgh).

A bird-cage belfry is the only external adornment at Torphichen Parish Kirk, built on the site of the nave of the preceptory of the Knights of the order of St John of Jerusalem and first used for worship in 1756. To the right of the door ascends an external stone stairway, which allows separate entrance to the laird's loft. This permitted the laird, his wife, their family and their entourage of servants to attend worship without having to pass through the crowded ranks of the local people in the pews below. The loft remains empty every Sunday as Lord Torphichen is an absentee landlord.

Displaced by Lord Torphichen, Henry Gillon of Wallhouse, who built Torphichen Parish Kirk with its laird's loft, had to make do with one of the side galleries which still bears his family's coat of arms as seen in this interior view of the 18th century church. The picture also shows the banners of the Knights of the Order of St John of Jerusalem, whose office holders such as sword bearer and standard bearer have their named stalls in the church. In the foreground are the font, the holy table and the lectern, all of which are decorated with the Order's distinctive eight-pointed Maltese Cross. Behind the communion table can be seen the steps that lead up to the pulpit, which is deliberately situated in the centre of the longest wall of the kirk. In true Presbyterian fashion, this allows as many of the congregation as possible to be close to the minister when he preaches and as near as possible to the Holy Table when he conducts communion. An interesting feature of this historic kirk is the pew which folds down to provide an additional long communion table.

A poster depicting the distinctive eight-pointed cross of the Order of the Knights of St John of Jerusalem advertises an exhibition about the life and work of the order in this picture of the twelth-century Preceptory. The Preceptory is famed as one of the few buildings in Scotland that is both military and ecclesiastic in design. Its defensive features, including the arrow slit windows in the tower and its roof top battlements are clearly visible. As a result of their military strength, the knights were able to offer the right of sanctuary not only within the walls of the church itself as in many other parts of Scotland, but also within a distance of one mile to the north, south, east and west. The boundaries of the sanctuary lands were marked distinctly by large tall standing stones. The distance is calculated from the central sanctuary stone in the churchyard, which bears the sign of the cross. However, the cup-like depression in this stone suggests that it may have had an older pagan use as a sacrificial altar; it may originally have been sited on the summit of nearby Cairnpapple Hill, where the Beaker Age Men had their settlement 2,000 years before the birth of Christ.

The exhibition staged by the Order of the Knights of St John of Jerusalem is seen in this interior view of the ancient preceptory with the visored figure of one of the Knights holding his pennant-decorated lance next to the banner. In the background below the tracery of the large window may be seen the lepers' squint. This was a small slanting window through which sufferers from the dreaded skin disease could witness worship without the danger of coming into contact with other members of the congregation and thus passing on their infection. The hospital in which the Knights treated the lepers and other patients at Torphichen was one of the earliest in Scotland. It is believed to have been situated in a three-storey block, which adjoined the existing north transept and was known as the Tenement. Evidence of the stone stair allowing those patients other than the lepers who were able to rise from their sick beds and descend into the church can still be seen.

Since the Order of St John of Jerusalem was re-established in Scotland in 1947, the knights have returned regularly to worship either in the ruins of the preceptory or in the adjoining church. Here they are seen during one of their earliest visits to the village in the 1950s progressing from St John's Hall across the village square.

The knights return annually on the final Sunday in August to worship in Torphichen.

The interior of the Preceptory, arranged for one of the annual services of the Knights of the Order of St John of Jerusalem. The preceptory's other historic claim to fame is as the place where Sir William Wallace, of *Braveheart* fame, met his nobles for the last time before they fought in the ill-fated Battle of Falkirk in 1298. After the defeat of Wallace and his Scottish followers, King Edward I of England, the so-called 'Hammer of the Scots', sought attention for his broken ribs at the knights' hospital at Torphichen. He had been injured during the night before the battle when, lying outside his tent because of the heat, he was accidentally trodden on by his battle charger. While he was receiving treatment, it is alleged that Wallace was in hiding in a cave on the banks of the River Avon.

The knights with their banner held high are seen leaving the Preceptory after worship. In the grounds of the preceptory can be seen the foundations of the monastery buildings in which the knights lived. They encircled the grassy central garth, where the younger knights were permitted to exercise by playing bowls and other games. The garth was surrounded by a covered cloister walk, where the knights prayed and meditated. Stones from this part of the monastery are preserved both built into the walls of the church and in a display in the upper rooms of the preceptory. Here there is also a small exhibition about the history of the order, which is the oldest order of chivalry in the world. Details of its present charitable works from supporting the modern eye hospital in Jerusalem to financing mountain rescue teams in various parts of Scotland are also illustrated.

A heavy snow fall lent a Christmas card aspect to this view of Torphichen Parish Church and Preceptory taken by Dr W. Anderson from the village square looking east along the Bowyett. The Bowyett takes its name from the old Scottish word for gate and from the bow butts, the small, rounded, grass-covered buttock-like hillocks on which the targets where the village men and boys in mediaeval times practised their archery skills were situated. The bow butts, like the little low-roofed cottages in the picture, have long since disappeared but the thick grey stone tower of the preceptory still dominates this picturesque village.

The season changes from the midwinter of the last pictures to the high summer crowning of Torphichen's gala queen, a ceremony which still takes place in the village every year on a Saturday in mid-June. This evocative Edwardian scene shows the coronation of the Torphichen schoolgirl queen in the crowded village square. Nowadays the ceremony is enacted in the more spacious setting of the primary school grounds, but otherwise many of the gala day royal court on the stage beside the flower-bedecked well still look familiar to a modern eye. The maypole around which the children at the foot of the steps are about to dance is however no longer a feature of the day's proceedings. Taken from the grounds of Glebe House, which was at this time still the home of the parish minister, this photograph also provides a fascinating glimpse of a time of change. Horse-drawn carriages were still the commonest form of transport, but one of the first cars in the district was nosing into the scene. The village store in the background, which in more recent years became an antique shop and is now a private house, belonged at this time to the well-known McNair family. As the sign above the left hand window indicates, they also ran a cab and carriage hire service and soon afterwards provided the village with its first motor charabanc service to Bathgate. Incongruous though it may seem to us, from the same premises the McNairs operated a flourishing licensed grocer's shop supplying villagers with wines, beers and spirits. Whilst McNair's store was operated by Bathgate Co-operative Society as a general store, later became an antique shop and is now a private home, the private cottage behind the gala day stage in the picture is now the village post office and one of its two well-stocked shops. Beyond the slate roof of the long low whitewashed building to the right of McNair's store can be glimpsed the roof and smoking chimneys of Rose Cottage, which was in those days the village smithy, where the farrier made horse shoes and the blacksmith repaired ploughs and other agricultural implements. It still stands, still has an open coal fire and is now the home of Mr Pender, whose son Gordon operates his joiner's business from the outhouses in its yard.

The oddly shaped square at Torphichen was also, more controversially, the place where the Linlithgow and Stirlingshire Hunt gathered before enjoying a day in the field, when hounds covered this part of its territory. The only building in this picture which remains standing is the late eighteenth-century block behind the well, which now houses the village post office and the general store known as Four Square at either end of it. Against the whitewashed walls of the two-storeyed part of the late eighteenth-century range of buildings can be seen a horse-drawn brake crowded with people who have arrived to watch the day's hunt. To the left of it the words painted on the wall between the first two dormer windows advertise the village coffee shop, with a lantern above its door to help pick it out for travellers arriving after dark. The lantern survives, but the coffee shop has for many years been a private house. The thoughts of most of the huntsmen and their followers on this crisp winter morning would anyway turn to something stronger, in the form of the stirrup cup. This would be filled and passed around by the licensee at the village inn, which was in those days known as the Burnside.

This view of Torphichen Square shows it in tranquil mood. Looking north along the Loan, the main road leading out of the village to Linlithgow, can be seen the entrance to the Fitzgerald Hall. Long demolished and replaced by the village community centre, but whose name is preserved in Fitzgerald Place where sheltered houses for senior citizens now stand. The open space in the foreground was known locally as 'nae place corner', after the reply of local youngsters when asked by their parents where they were going.

The village children at one time received both primary and secondary education at Torphichen School. These classrooms of 1895 are still in use beyond the wrought-iron railings, along with a classroom erected in 1958 on the right. The school in fact existed well before the Victorian era; its infant room, which is concealed in this photograph, dates from the eighteenth century. The carving of the Biblical burning bush on its facade with the Latin motto New Tamen Consebatur ('Yet never Consumed'), which is the symbol and motto of the Church of Scotland, suggests that it was originally built by the Church. Carvings of the heads of two figures adorn either side of the window of the infant classroom but their identity is a mystery.

Torphichen School's most famous former pupil was Henry Bell, son of the village miller who was originally apprenticed to his father but went on to serve a second apprenticeship as a shipwright at the Bo'ness shipbuilding yard of Shaw & Hart. He later proposed steam power as a means of propulsion to the Admiralty, where only Lord Nelson took him seriously. He privately financed and built the world's first practical seagoing steamship, the *Comet*. Here is seen the original plaster cast of Bell's famous pioneering little vessel, prepared for the memorial bronze tablet placed on the gable wall of Torphichen Mill. Below are the medals, one bearing an effigy of the famous inventor, which were given by his proud descendants to Torphichen Primary and other West Lothian Schools for presentation to their dux pupils on the occasion of Bell's centenary. The memorial at the mill on the banks of the River Avon where Bell spent his childhood was unveiled in the afternoon of 4 November 1911 by Professor Hundson Beare of Edinburgh University, who provided the text about Henry Bell for the Encylopedia Britannica.

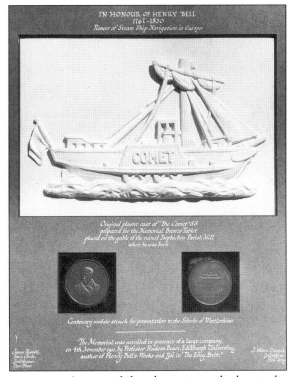

A copy of the plaque is on display in the village kirk, where it was unveiled by famous Clyde shipyard director, Ross Belch.

In 1970 these pupils of Torphichen Primary were encouraged to experiment like Bell. During a session of the school's popular afternoon club they were supervised by a parent volunteer, who also brought along her young son to join the older boys in the senior classroom overlooking The Loan.

Many Torphichen parents (including Mrs Mamie Wolfe and Mrs Jane MacKenzie) gave up their time to help with the school club.

Painting was a popular activity at club time at Torphichen Primary, here supervised by Mrs Lily Mitchell.

During this period Torphichen Primary School even had its own donkey Thomasina, gifted to the pupils by Mr and Mrs Wishart of Glebe House, in whose grounds this photograph was taken.

Another popular outdoor activity with the pupils at Torphichen Primary was mapping and here a group of the girls are seen busy at work in the Bowyett. In the background is the school's new dining room and kitchen where the cook, Mrs Hettie Wallace, every school day produced hearty home-made soup, steak pie, mince and tatties and other traditional fare which the children ate under the supervision of Mrs Nancy Watson. In the 1970s the school roll at Torphichen Primary included many children from Wallhouse Children's Home, who appreciated particularly the homely atmosphere in which these ladies helped create and made them welcome during their temporary stays.

This picture shows the new dining hall at Torphichen Primary before the building of the adjacent community centre hall. In the background can be seen the Preceptory tower and to the left are the Giant's Knuckles, as the five ridged hills behind the village are known from their resemblance to the back of a huge hand.

In 1969 and 1970 the pupils of Torphichen Primary took part in two school musical shows. This picture shows the cast of the first of these productions, in which Scottish National Party Parliamentary candidate Douglas Henderson's daughter Fiona played the title role of Alice in an adaptation of Lewis Carroll's book.

Jackie Reynolds, a descendant of Lord Beaverbrook who had many connections with Torphichen, played the role of the Artful Dodger, in the school's memorable production of Charles Dicken's classic, Oliver Twist. Here she is seen with the boys and girls of Fagin's pickpocketing gang.

The success of Alice led to an even more ambitious staging of Oliver Twist the following year with Jane Barrowcliffe as young Oliver and Jackie Reynolds as a confident, cocky Artful Dodger. Here they are seen with the entire cast of the show on the crowded stage in the school's tiny assembly hall.

School club and school shows still left time for class work at Torphichen Primary and here four of the school's younger pupils are seen in the reading corner with a collage which they had made on the wall behind them.

Lack of space at Torphichen Primary School led to this cloakroom being pressed into use as the school library. One of the pupils, Jane Barrowcliffe, seen earlier in her role as Oliver Twist, later went on to make a career as a school librarian.

A corner at Torphichen Primary was also found for the school shop where pupils practised arithmetic by buying and selling the goods on the shelves.

An open reel-to-reel tape recorder was operated alongside the latest innovation, a cassette tape recorder, during this lesson at Torphichen Primary School in 1970. As well as producing their own radio programmes, the pupils were proud of their school newspaper and magazine, The Comet. In this picture, older pupil Aileen Kerr was overseeing the work of younger pupils. Future school librarian Jane Barrowcliffe is the girl in the middle behind the tape recorder.

Wallhouse, Torphichen.

Many of the pupils who attended Torphichen Primary School in the decades prior to 1980 were residents of the children's home which then occupied Wallhouse House, pictured here in Edwardian days when it was still a private house. Wallhouse takes its name from the well where the Knights of St John obtained their fresh water, a scene depicted in the stained glass window that adorns the main stair well. For over three centuries, the Wallhouse estate belonged to the same family, the Gillons, one of whose number Henry provided the £300 necessary to provide Torphichen with a new kirk. The present Victorian-style house was built in 1846 and on the facade above the main entrance is carved the coat of arms of the Gillon family. The ravens depicted on it are a reminder that Torphichen is derived from the Celtic *tor* meaning hill and *phichen* meaning ravens or magpies. The Gillon family motto 'Protection and Refuge' is also a reminder of the right of sanctuary operated by the Knights of St John, which took in the lands occupied by the Wallhouse Estate. Several of the Gillons followed distinguished military careers and mention of them can be found on plaques in Torphichen Kirk and on the impressive family gravestone in the churchyard. After the Gillons moved south to live in England, where several of their descendants live still, Wallhouse was acquired by local Armadale colliery owner Mr James Wood of Bathville. He gifted the playing field to Torphichen and in addition gave permission for the village gala day to hold its sports in the grounds of his home, as seen in this photograph. After the Second World War Wallhouse was acquired by West Lothian County Council and converted into a children's home. When, by the 1980s, such large institutional homes had become unfashionable as increasing numbers of children in need of care and protection were fostered, it was proposed that Wallhouse should become an old folks' home or a hospice for those suffering from AIDS. Neither of these ideas came to fruition and instead the house became the headquarters for a business concern, which also attempted to establish it as a conference centre. Now the old house is happily back in private ownership and several other attractive homes have been built in the former walled garden. The Gaelic version of its name, Tighballa, has also been adopted by the successful restaurant that has been established on the site of the former clay mine on the western edge of the estate.

Another glimpse of an early Torphichen gala day is provided by this photograph of the winning entry in the competition for decorated house frontages, which is still a feature of present day galas. Also surely worthy of a prize was the flower-adorned hat worn by the lady holding the baby, while the clothes worn by the other onlookers give a detailed glimpse of the fashions of the period. It is interesting to note that even the youngest of the boys wear caps or hats; perhaps the thickness of their serge suits provides an explanation as to why summer days were reportedly warmer in those bygone days. The little girls are all arrayed in their best summer dresses with frills and flounces much in evidence and in the case of two of them pantalettes peeping out below their hemlines. One of the little girls wears black stockings but the others have bare legs and like the boys all except one wears buttoned boots.

As well as decorated house frontages, the residents of Torphichen took pride in each year building a large arch to mark the occasion of the gala day. This one covered in green boxwood was erected in 1910 at the junction of High Brae with the village square.

48

SLACKEND. TORPHICHEN.   R.BRAID. Photo.

Slackend House, now known as Craigs House, and the steading buildings of the former Slackend Farm still stand on opposite sides of the main road at Slackend Cross Roads as pictured in this postcard view taken by Livingston photographer Robert Braid. These days the road is much busier than when the two men stopped for a blether right in the middle of it. Slackend House was originally owned by Bathgate lawyer Mr A.K. Fleming. With its surrounding trees it looks little changed from when it belonged to the Simpson family, of whom Sir James Young Simpson of chloroform fame was a descendant. The Simpsons originally came to Torphichen as a Huguenot family who had fled from religious persecution in France. Despite their strong non-conformist beliefs, the Simpsons were a superstitious family and on his childhood visits to Slackend young James Simpson is said to have listened in fascination to the many tales of the supernatural which he was told. One concerned his grandfather, who returned to the farmhouse one day to learn that a gypsy girl, turned away empty handed by a farm servant, had put a curse on it. Furious he set off in pursuit and finding her sitting on the step of the coffee house in Torphichen Square, grabbed hold of her and with his knife scratched a cross on the brow of her face as the only way to ensure that the curse was removed. Farmer Simpson was one of those in the Torphichen area who believed that the countryside was haunted by the evil Lord of Murain, who seized every opportunity to creep into the earth of the fields and poison it. When ploughing he therefore never left the end of a furrow open but always carefully turned it into the next one. Despite this precaution, when his herd of cattle fell ill the old man was convinced that the wicked spirit of the soil was responsible. In desperation, to appease the Lord of Murrain he is said to have dug a deep pit, led a healthy cow into it and buried it alive as a sacrifice. On a lighter note, farmer Simpson's superstitious nature also made him very wary of black cats. He did not like to have any about the steading at Slackend as he believed that they were witches' familiars and not at all the symbol of good luck they are considered nowadays. He also believed the crazy antics of the mad March hares, at mating time, to be an ill omen. If he saw one in his fields while going to market in Linlithgow or Bathgate he would turn round and go home, convinced he would not obtain a good price for his goods that day.

The site of the coffee house in the square at Torphichen is still marked by the lantern on the doorstep, below which Farmer Simpson found the gypsy girl who cursed his land. In the forefront is the red sandstone well constructed in 1897 as the village's way of marking Queen Victoria's Diamond Jubilee (although there had of course been a source of fresh water at this site for centuries before the royal anniversary). The plaque on the side of the well depicts the elderly Queen as she looked after sixty years on the British throne, around it are the names of the countries of the British Empire of which she was the proud ruler and, in the case of India, Empress.

The annual Sunday School picnic was another highlight of summer in Torphichen. The children and their teachers were conveyed on a fleet of horse-drawn hay carts to local beauty spots such as Bridge Castle, near Westfield, and Caribber Glen, whose grassy slopes ran down to the shores of the River Avon. All of the farmers whose fields surrounded the village lent their large wheeled carts and Clydesdale horses to provide the transport for this outing, which was always held on a Saturday in late June or early July. The horses' leather harnesses were always specially polished and decorated for the occasion. The gentleman on foot with the walking stick was parish minister Rev. Mr Beale, whose spectacles glinted in the sunshine. The following Sunday at morning service in Torphichen Kirk, he would present books as prizes to those children who had achieved good attendance at Sunday School and church throughout the year.

Torphichen post office is now in the Square, but in earlier years it was housed in one of the downstairs rooms of Green Cottage next to the village playing field in the Loan. Notices giving postal information can be seen in the window on the right. Green Cottage was originally a single-storeyed building and the change in the colour of the stone indicates where the upstairs bedrooms were later added. The cottage is now a private home.

The High Brae in Torphichen is pictured here at the beginning of the 1900s before the road was surfaced – the homes that line it are still recognisable. The buildings are all typical of Scottish domestic architecture with the roofs of the two cottages on the left covered in red pantiles and those of the other two houses covered in grey slates. The stonework of the late Georgian two-storeyed house in the middle has been left exposed but the walls of its neighbours on either side have been harled. The application of harling was like giving a house a winter overcoat to protect it from the weathering effects of wind and rain, in particular to stop water entering the stonework and freezing thus causing damage when it expanded. Below High Brae runs Low Brae, along the length of which are several cottages whose walls are harled with crushed sea shells; as well as protecting them this gives an attractive appearance. Brae is a Scottish word derived from Gaelic meaning a hill, which is an excellent description for these two narrow roads as they snake steeply up from Torphichen Square and lead to Manse Road.

The caption on this postcard states High Brae, but it actually depicts Manse Road looking north towards the top of Low Brae, where the single-storeyed cottage has been replaced by two-storeyed St John's House. As the caption also indicates the front facade and the little belfry of St John's Church can be seen. The building still stands but is now the hall for Torphichen Kirk and the belfry with its weather vane has sadly been removed. The church bell is presently on display in Torphichen Kirk. The manse from which the road now takes its name is situated to the left of St John's Hall. It dates from the 1940s and is occupied by the parish minister, whose original home was the now privately owned Glebe House. The word glebe meant the minister's garden, in which he was expected to grow vegetables to supplement his meagre annual stipend. The old cottages on the left have been replaced by more modern ones, but the scene has otherwise changed little a century later.

St John's has a special place in Scottish ecclesiastical history as it was the first stone Free Church, built only months after the Disruption which split the Church of Scotland at its General Assembly in 1843. Many of its ministers and elders, led by the Rev. Thomas Chalmers of Anstruther, who was related to the Linlithgow Bridge paper mill owning family, marched out of St Andrew's Church in George Street, Edinburgh. They were protesting at the church establishment's continued support for the right of lairds to decide who should preach in their parishes. The divide in the congregation at Torphichen lasted until 1929 when moves were made throughout Scotland to heal the breach. In Torphichen, well-respected parish minister the Rev. Hugh P.R. Mackay succeeded in persuading villagers that they should once again unite in worship in the kirk and that St John's should become the church hall. The gateway on the left now leads to the modern manse.

Four

Bathgate:
The Old Town

Whilst nowhere in Bathgate can compete with the antiquity of Torphichen's twelfth-century Preceptory, the origins of the town can still be traced around the site of the High Kirk whose Victorian building replaced one built in 1739. Textiles formed the predominant industry at this time, with the weavers producing cloth from looms in their own homes. Many of the weavers are believed to have come originally from France. Like the Simpsons mentioned in the previous chapter, they fled as Protestant Huguenots from Catholic persecution to freedom. The local place name Jarvey Street is said to derive from one of these immigrant French families, the Jarves. It is, however, the Simpsons who are best known, thanks to the talent of son James. He became Scotland's most famous nineteenth-century surgeon as a result of his pioneering work in the field of anaesthesia. Simpson was born in 1812 in a house in Main Street in the shadow of the old High Kirk. His father owned a bakery in the town and from a young age Simpson helped delivered the morning rolls and later in the day ran round the houses again knocking on doors with orders of bread and tea breads such as scones and pancakes. Amongst the homes at which he called regularly was the big house, Balbardie House, which was the home of Bathgate's first Provost, Alexander Marjoribanks. Provost Marjoribanks soon got to know the little delivery boy and, impressed by his brightness and the searching questions which he lingered to ask, nicknamed him the 'Young Philosopher'. Other customers also noted the laddie's obvious intelligence and they in turn called him, 'The Box o' Brains', while at school the master acknowledged him as, 'The Wise Wean', 'The Wise Wee One'. The dominie, Mr Henderson, had his nickname too, being called by his pupils 'Timmerleg' on account of the fact that his leg had been amputated, forcing him to hobble around the classroom on a wooden limb. This happened long before the discovery of chloroform by his cleverest pupil, which would have saved him from terrible pain.

This rare view shows the house on the left hand side of Main Street, where Sir James Young Simpson was born in 1812 and lived until he left home at the age of only fourteen to become a student in the medical faculty at the University of Edinburgh. The crowded old houses in Main Street survived the construction of the new High Church whose tower is seen looming over them, but most were demolished during improvements to the town during the early years of the twentieth century.

Bathgate's original High Church, which stood on the same hilltop site as the present one ,was completed in 1739. Its long rectangular shaped building was very typical of the church architecture of its period, with the small bell tower at the West End in strict Presbyterian style its only external adornment. It had a grey slate roof and its stone walls were harled to protect them from the effects of the weather. It had two entrances set at the west and east ends of its south wall, facing the graveyard. Two small windows at either end lit the steep stairs to the lofts or galleries which spanned each end of the interior and were in turn illuminated by small windows on both the south and north walls. Most of the light in the church came from the pair of two storey high, long, narrow windows that faced the pulpit situated in the centre of the north wall. The interior was as plain as the exterior. Apart from the paupers' pew directly below the pulpit, all of the seats had doors and seat rents had to be paid quarterly by members of the congregation who sat there. The original church was demolished to make way for the new church in 1883.

One strange relic from the original Bathgate High Church survives as an exhibit in the Bennie Museum. Pictured here in its original setting in the kirk, it is the infamous 'seat of repentance' or the 'cutty stool' as it was more commonly known. It was used in a variety of ways for the punishment of erring members of the congregation, at the direction of the Kirk Session. As a court of the church, the elders with the minister as their chairman or moderator still meet regularly, but until the end of the nineteenth century wielded far greater power than they do today. Moral omissions of their fellow parishioners they sought to punish through public exposure, by making them sit on the cutty stool. These sins ranged from repeated absence from worship to chattering or worse still falling asleep during the minister's lengthy sermons and from swearing to fornication. For those who were found to have dared to have sex outside of marriage, an unusual feature of the Bathgate seat was that it was designed so that both partners could be shamed at the same time. As they sat together, further attention was often focused on them by setting the seat on a raised dais and making them wear white linen gowns. Much more painful was the fate of the children of the congregation who, if they were deemed to have misbehaved, were ordered to bend over the middle section. So positioned, their buttocks were raised for the Kirk Session's officer the Beadle to whip them with painful strokes of the birch rod.

Amongst the buildings in the old town of Bathgate looking west along Jarvey Street is the town jail, which is seen in the background on the left. Those punished in its grim dark cells were usually sentenced at the Burgh Court at which the Bailies, the town's three magistrates, presided weekly. The court usually met on Monday morning to deal with those arrested for being drunk and disorderly or committing a public nuisance on the previous Saturday night. Other crimes punished regularly at the Burgh Court ranged from petty theft to domestic violence. While adults were either fined or sentenced to a number of days in jail, delinquent boys were served immediately with sentences of corporal punishment. These were administered in the presence of the parents by one of the local police constables with an official birch rod which was both longer and heavier than that wielded by the church Beadle. Thrashings ranged from three strokes for repeatedly playing truant from school to as many as twelve for theft.

The 108ft tower of the High Church built in 1884 rises high over the north side of Jarvey Street in this postcard view. Designed in Norman style with its square tower adorned with pinnacles it cost £8000 to build. Its bell was gifted by former Provost John Waddell at a cost of £250. Its clock is set at a level of ninety feet so that it can be seen from a wide area. A pipe organ was installed in 1899.

This photograph shows the view looking down directly from the top of the tower of the High Church into Brown Square or the Bunker, as it was known because of its tight trench-like shape. Beyond the roofs of the houses lay the lawns and grounds of Balbardie House, a part of which can be see at the top of the picture.

Balbardie House was the mansion home of the Marjoribanks family, one of whom, Alexander, was Bathgate's first Provost and the man who organised the campaign to ensure the building of the Academy. Balbardie House was demolished many years ago but the name is preserved in that of Balbardie Primary School. It is said to mean the woods of the wild boar and when in residence at Linlithgow Palace, Scotland's kings and queens and their royal courtiers are said to have enjoyed excellent hunting in this area.

This fine view of Jarvey Street looking north shows the High Church tower rising high over the roof of one of the town's principal public buildings, the Corn Exchange. Each week the Corn Exchange was where local farmers sold their grain and other crops by public auction. The large hall where the auctions took place was also used in the evenings as the scene for dinners and dances and became the hub of Bathgate's social life. Its entertainment role outlived its life as an auction house and for many years local young people enjoyed meeting there. When renamed the Palais it was the scene of regular dances every weekend. As tastes in dance music changed the Palais became the Queen's Disco.

The Lodge Torphichen Kilwinning No.13 met from 1736, and built these premises in 1736 in Gideon Street. The present Masonice Lodge in Jarvey Street was built in 1902.

JARVEY STREET, BATHGATE

Looking in the opposite direction towards Marjoribanks Street, the horse-drawn cart waiting patiently on the right and the large number of children standing in the roadway all add interest to this other view of Jarvey Street.

This attractive old building with its bow front, pantiled roof and fore stairs leading up to the first floor entrance once stood in Jarvey Street. It was demolished to make way for the construction of the headquarters for Bathgate Co-operative Society including its hall which to a large extent replaced the Corn Exchange opposite as the centre of the town's social scene. Known for many years as the Speyside Suite, the Co-op Hall was the setting for a wide array of events from joyful wedding receptions to sad funeral purveys. It was also the venue for most of the town's annual dinner dances in the days before hotels took over the catering. Many memorable Burns Suppers were held in its first floor rooms before it was finally destroyed in a disastrous blaze which damaged the premises so extensively that they had to be demolished.

59

A Bit of Old Bathgate

This very early postcard of Cochrane Street shows two girls pushing a baby in a pram as ladies enjoy a stroll down the middle of the traffic-free road. The small single-storeyed cottages were typical of the homes occupied by Bathgate's weavers that even by the time this view was taken were being replaced by the type of tenement building seen on the left. The whitewashed building on the opposite side of the street was a dairy. Beyond it the two-storeyed building was known as Cochrane View and in the far distance were the malt barns.

Another very early postcard, entitled simply 'A Bit of Old Bathgate', is also believed to be of the top end of Cochrane Street.

The Simpson Memorial Church is a modern building which stands in the old part of Bathgate near to where the famous surgeon was born and raised. After successfully completing his studies at the University of Edinburgh Simpson became a member of the city's famous Royal College of Surgeons when he was still only eighteen years old. This was deemed too young to grant him the degree of Doctor of Medicine, despite the fact that a year earlier he had saved the life of a patient. To fill in time until he was recognised and could practise, he went to the docks at Leith to try to find a post as a ship's surgeon, but no vessel would accept him because of his youth. Simpson therefore came home to Bathgate for a while where he stayed in the old house belonging to his brother.

Bathgate's only other tribute to its most famous son comes in the shape of these name plaques at the entrances to the town. After he became successful, rich and very famous Sir James returned to Bathgate on several occasions, causing a great impression amongst the local folk with his splendid horses and carriage. In 1861 he visited Bathgate Academy where he presented a silver thimble to be competed for annually and awarded to the girl who was best at sewing. This was a tribute to his sister Mary, to whom during his student days he admitted having dispatched many bundles of stockings for darning. Mary was Simpson's only sister and he also recalled his great affection for her when he reminded the audience how at Edinburgh University he had won the Stuart Bursary. He had immediately rushed out to spend part of the £10 which it was worth to buy her a tippet, a long length of best quality cloth which she wore as a shawl.

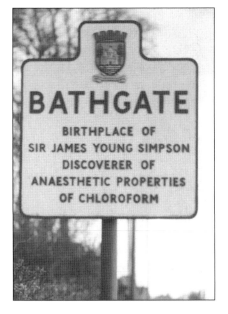

Muir Road Bridgend

Gradually the tight knit old town of Bathgate began to expand as this picture postcard photograph of Muir Road looking east towards the outline of the Bathgate Hills shows. The families who occupied its solidly built, slate-roofed stone homes with their ranks of chimney pots for coal fires were large, as can be seen from the crowd of white pinafore clad girls standing by the wrought-iron railings in front of the corner cottage.

Long before the coming of supermarkets such as Tesco, Lidl and Aldi, corner shops such as this one at the Glasgow Road end of Mill Road served all the requirements of the families who lived within walking distance of them in the decades when very few people owned cars. 'Going the messages' was a regular daily family chore for many bairns who to make the errand more fun often used to run from their homes to the shop trundling their gird, a noisy iron hoop. Girls' girds had the long iron cleek with which they were pushed attached to them, but boys' thought that this was 'cissy' as it made the control of the gird too easy. Their girds and cleeks were therefore separate with simply a small hook on the side of the hoop for the cleek to catch as they birled it along the street. Once they reached the shop and bought their purchases, perhaps they would be rewarded by being allowed to spend the change on some of the Fry's chocolate advertised on the corner window. The little corner shop also sold newspapers as the headlines on the advertising placards at the door indicate, but the boys and girls were probably more interested in the array of weekly illustrated comics which it also stocked.

Some of the oldest houses in Bathgate stood at Guildy Haugh Toll. This photograph was taken by Robert Braid and published from his studio in Livingston where his premises can still be seen in the village main street.

Housing in Bathgate changed dramatically in the late 1920s with the building of the first council houses, which were made available to rent at very economical weekly rates. Typical were these brick built harled two-storeyed three and four apartment homes in Stewart Terrace. With their separate bedrooms for the parents and children, their indoor bathrooms and kitchens with running water, they were very modern in comparison with the cottage homes in the above picture. Occupation of them was thought a just reward for the many men who had fought for their country during the First World War. A feature of the new houses built by Bathgate Town Council was that they all had both front and back gardens where their inhabitants could grow their own flowers and vegetables. Since the 1980s, the law has allowed tenants to purchase their homes.

Five

Bathgate at Work

Bathgate's main claim to fame as an industrial centre is as the site of the world's first oil refinery. This came about in 1848 when a young Glasgow born scientist, James Young, obtained a site at Whiteside near Whitburn Road where he built retorts to obtain oil from coal which he mined locally at Torbanehill. Until then the main source of oil was from the fatty blubber of whales caught in the Arctic Sea. The oil thus obtained was usable in lamps, but was not of sufficiently high quality to lubricate the growing number of machines coming into use as a result of the Industrial Revolution. Young's interest in producing oil from coal came about from experiments that he carried out while working as an assistant to the professor of chemistry at Glasgow University. He continued these at the University of London and during his time in the commercial sector working at a chemical plant in Manchester. It was at the latter that he made use of the Penny Post, only established in 1840, to send out a whole series of letters to his former classmates at Glasgow's Andersen Institute, now the University of Strathclyde, where as a young student he had attended night school. In his letters he asked them to send him samples of coal from the areas where they now worked. Amongst those who replied was Hugh Bartholomew, the manager of a gas works. In an accompanying note, he stated that the fuel he burnt at his plant came from Boghead Pit between Bathgate and Armadale. The miners who dug it nicknamed it 'parrot or cannel coal' because when they burned it on their own fires it spluttered making a noise like a chattering parrot, while at the same time giving off a light which was as bright as any candle. When Young set light to the sample he found that it more than lived up to Bartholomew's claims and as oil oozed out, he realised that it was by far the richest of the coals he had tested. He wasted no time in travelling to Bathgate where he quickly concluded a deal with the owner of what became known as the Torbanehill Mineral. It was an agreement that later led to a long running legal battle, but which at the same time effectively founded the oil industry in Scotland, long before that of America or anywhere else in the world.

As Bathgate grew as a coal mining and oil-producing centre, the surrounding area also attracted other heavy industries including iron, steel and brick making. For a century they kept the men of Bathgate hard at work, while their wives continued the town's links with the textile trade. However, by the 1950s most were in decline as Scotland faced post-Second World War industrial expansion and competition from overseas producers. It was at this time that the British

Government under its controversial relocation policy decided to try to give West Lothian, which was at the time the poorest part of Scotland, a boost by encouraging British Leyland to establish a new truck and tractor plant there. Blackburn, with its vacant acres of flat land, was chosen as the ideal site for the erection of the long construction line that the new British Motor Corporation plant required. As soon as the enormous BMC factory was completed, overspill families were encouraged to leave Glasgow to come to live in Blackburn and provide labour for the new works which were seen as a symbol of hope for the whole of Scotland. Almost as soon as they arrived, however, BMC with its 5,000-strong work force began to experience problems on both management and trade union sides. Basically, the new works were sited too far away from the rest of the industry in the Midlands of England. Separated by 300 miles from its ancillary suppliers, communication problems resulted in a lack of the continuity which the construction line required to ensure maximum economic production. At the same time, overseas orders for the large tractors which the Bathgate works was producing failed to reach expectations and soon BMC's short life was at an end. Its closure was another severe blow to the whole of West Lothian. Yet after a period of high unemployment, the area has fought back and is now the proud capital of Scotland's 'Silicon Glen' with top firms from such asNEC all offering highly paid jobs.

Inventor James Young founded the Bathgate Oil Refinery in 1851 and proved as good a businessman as he was scientist by protecting the processes perfected there with patents. He was nicknamed 'Paraffin Young', due to the success of his main product which revolutionised the standard of lighting in homes. He was always proud of the fact that his much safer and efficient lamps made it much easier for young Scots to read and study. Young quickly expanded his mineral oil business by shifting from the limited supplies of Torbanehill Mineral to the much more easily sourced shale, and by building oil works in neighbouring places such as Broxburn, Pumpherston, Livingston Station and Addiewell to utilise it. Meanwhile, he entrusted the management of the Bathgate refinery to his partner, Edward Meldrum, on whose estate at Deans near Livingston the primary school which bears his name now stands. His name is also remembered on the site of the original refinery by Meldrum Cottage, the only building still in standing.

At the time of the opening of the new oil refinery at the end of the 1840s, Bathgate's main industry was the production of textiles, with the cloth being manufactured on looms in the workers' own homes. Nisbet Easton, who posed for this photograph by his kitchen range, was known as 'the last of the Bathgate weavers'. As he waits for the kettle on top of the stove to boil to make a pot of tea, old Nisbet has an open book on the table by his side. This is a fitting reminder that while the Bathgate weavers worked with their hands they also were largely self-taught. They used their brains not only to create the designs which they so patiently wove, but also, after their day's work was over, to take part in the town's famous Under The Beeches Literary Society, founded in 1874. Several of those involved in the textile trade were also poets, including craftsman John Stark who produced handmade spinning wheels. 'Starkie', as he was known, was inspired by his admiration for the works of Robert Burns, and on the bard's birthday on 25 January, always decorated his cottage and held open house to welcome other local enthusiasts to share in the reading and reciting of the poet's works. Old Starkie was also popular with the town's children as he made wooden peeries, spinning tops with which they loved to play.

Bathgate continued to be involved in the textile trade throughout much of the twentieth century. This wonderfully evocative photograph of working conditions in one of the town's hosieries was taken in the 1920s, on the workshop floor of Livingston's Hosiery in Gardner's Lane. The building was later taken over by Dacoll.

This rare view shows the result of an explosion at Balbardie Colliery in Torphichen Street. The colliery, which was one of many small coal pits around Bathgate, was first opened in 1892. The underground workings honeycomb much of the Bathgate area and still cause problems with subsidence. In recent years the last remains of the coal industry, the black pit bings of waste spoil, have been gradually reclaimed. Bathgate's Peace Park with its fine public golf course occupies the site of the Balbardie Colliery bing, a word derived from the Gaelic word 'ben', meaning mountain.

An early aerial view of part of Bathgate shows the Hopetoun Steel Works operated by Renton and Fisher. It manufactured many products required by the local coal and shale industries. Its two tall chimney stacks used to loom over the houses far below in Cochrane Street and Mill Road. Mill Road took its name from the grain mill which has been run for many years by the Chapman family. At the top of the photograph, the open space was the site of Mill Park football field. The railway line that snakes its way across the picture ran to Bathgate Lower Station and the main line north to Manual Junction on the Edinburgh to Glasgow line near Polmont.

Bathgate was served by two passenger railway stations, Bathgate Lower, which is illustrated here, and Bathgate Upper. Here a steam engine waits to pull a passenger train out of the station when signalled by the two railway company officials standing on the platform. Behind them can be seen the booking office and waiting room with its canopy jutting out over the platform. Rising behind its slated roof is one of the two tall chimneys mentioned in the previous caption and the second chimney at Renton and Fishers can be spotted on the opposite side of the tracks sticking out behind the clump of trees.

Bathgate Upper Station on a busy morning during the early 1920s, as a long passenger train steams below the footbridge and alongside the platform to embark the waiting workers. The wood-edged canopies covering both platforms are typical of Scottish railway architecture of the period. It is also interesting to study the clothes worn by the men waiting to board the incoming train. Dark suited, they all have flat caps or bowler hats and the one nearest the camera is sporting a gold watch chain. The predominance of men catching this early morning train to the city is a visual reminder that at this time a woman's place was still considerd to be as wife and mother in the home. A few girls did however travel every weekday to and from Bathgate by train as they were amongst the pupils from Fauldhouse who had passed their Qualifying examination to attend Bathgate Academy, which was at this time a selective school offering a specialised academic curriculum.

Bathgate's passenger railway service was a victim of the famous axe wielded by Lord Beeching, and passenger services to the town were withdrawn in January 1956. Almost forty years later a successful campaign was mounted and Bathgate was one of the first places to regain its passenger rail service, although only to Edinburgh and not Glasgow (originally linked via Airdrie). The single line operation to Edinburgh via Livingston North, Uphall Station and Haymarket is provided mainly by single unit diesel trains which take just under half an hour to complete the journey to Waverley Station. The train waiting to leave the platform at the newly-constructed station is seen from the large car park that has tempted many commuters to use this route. There is a smaller car park on the opposite side of the track in King Street. It was also used as a bus stop and is seen in the following photograph.

Passengers about to board one of the diesel hauled trains from Bathgate to Edinburgh, on a bright autumn Saturday morning in September 1999. To the south and west the new railway station is bounded by several large shops.

One of the main users of the railway system in Victorian times was the Royal Mail, which has operated its services from several post office premises in the town. The first post office in Bathgate opened in 1800 with Mr R. Mochrie as its postmaster. For the year ending 5 January 1803, Mr Mochrie's salary was £8. He hand franked all of the letters and parcels posted from the town; Bathgate's first postmark was a circular one containing the letters BATH and GATE printed one below the other. Mr Mochrie was succeeded in 1814 by John Jamieson, who held the post until 1830. This photograph shows the post office situated below the slated turret in Hopetoun Street in later Victorian times.

Smartly turned out in their navy blue uniforms with their peaked caps, the members of staff of Bathgate Post Office pose for the photographer outside its premises in Hopetoun Street. The size of the all-male staff is a reminder of what an important service it provided in the days before telephones were commonly available. Every day except Sunday there were three deliveries, two in the morning and one in the afternoon. For even speedier service it was possible to send a telegraph message and the four young telegraph boys are seen in the front row in this picture. They had to be fit as they were supplied with official royal mail bicycles on which to rush to deliver urgent messages to homes throughout the town. Often the bright yellow telegram forms they carried bore tidings of births, marriages and deaths.

The post office later moved to a more central site in George Square. The attractive turreted Scottish baronial style two-storeyed building with its grey slate roof and white harled walls was later acquired as a branch by the Royal Bank of Scotland when the post office moved to the more modern premises in North Bridge Street where it is still situated. There was also a sorting office at this new site, but this has now been moved to an out of town site where traffic congestion is less of a problem.

In its day Bathgate Co-operative Society was every bit as much an institution in the town as the post office. The Co-op or the Store was much more than a shop. It was a whole way of life for the majority of the people who lived in Bathgate, because they were all members of the society with therefore a direct interest in the level of its annual profits. To ensure that they received their fair share of the profits, members exchanged their cash for Co-op cheques, small discs in different colours to denote their value, and all cheques purchased were carefully listed both in the members chequebooks and in a master ledger. Purchases on credit were allowed but all debts had to be squared by the end of each of the quarters into which the trading year was divided. The final week of each quarter was often a difficult time for local families as they struggled to clear their debts and became known as 'the Lord Is My Shepherd Week' as the following line in the famous psalm states, 'I shall not want'. The size of dividend that the Co-op Board felt able to declare depended on how prosperous trade had been. It was often two shillings (10p) for every pound spent., but sometimes the loyalty of local families was rewarded with a bonanza as high as three shillings in the pound. Bathgate Co-op had its headquarters in Jeffrey Street and this picture shows its drapery and bakery departments. One of the two white-aproned assistants standing outside the door later became Mrs Brodie, whose husband started the well-known bakery in George Street – famous for its delicious hot apple and rhubarb tarts.

One of Bathgate Co-operative Society's large fleet of horse-drawn vehicles outside its premises, which were decorated for Newland's Day when this photograph was taken. Bathgate Co-op provided a daily delivery service of all essentials from early morning milk, rolls and bran scones to afternoon tea breads such as scones, pancakes and plain, iced and cream cookies. It also delivered groceries such as butter and cheese, fruit and vegetables and butcher meat. In the days before refrigerators, and with far fewer deep freezes, these items were purchased on a daily basis so that they were fresh. Notice the white-aproned shop assistants who came to the door of their premises and the crowd of small boys who gathered round to pose for the photographer.

For many years Bathgate Co-operative Society refused, as a matter of principle, to sell wines beers or spirits. Despite the Co-op's opposition, however, other merchants happily sold alcoholic beverages, and beer and whisky were both produced locally in Bathgate. During Victorian times there were as many as five breweries in the town with the three main ones being in Chapel Lane, Cochrane Street and Engine Street. The earliest known brewer was Shaw in the eighteenth century. The brewery in Cochrane Street, whose malt barns can be seen in an earlier picture, was owned by Robert Boyd. The brewery in Chapel Lane was operated until 1856 by James Wallace, when he let it to Thomas Robertson, who in turn appears to have moved the business to Engine Street where it closed in 1867. This picture shows The Glen, the home of the manager of McNab's Glenmavis Distillery, which continued to operate until the late 1950s on its site in Torphichen Road. The house still overlooks this scene but the rest of the site is now occupied by People's garage and car showrooms. This postcard was published before the First World War by J. Davidson, the well-known newsagents which still does business in Jarvey Street.

Dougall's Iron Foundry is seen in this early aerial photograph of the Mill Road area of Bathgate. Wolfe's Shovel Works were situated further long the street. On the railway line, an old signal box can be seen where it controlled the level crossing. The Bathgate Hills rise in the background, but it is interesting to note that the fields came right down into the town and that neatly built haystacks are visible in the field on the left.

Traditional tidily thatched haystacks can be seen in more detail in this beautiful view of Kirkton Kiln Farm on Puir Wife's Brae. How Puir Wife's Brae acquired its unusual name is a mystery that often arouses local controversy. This scene looks one of rural tranquillity, but through the trees the spread of housing can be glimpsed and nowadays only the place name remains as a lasting reminder of this more peaceful time in Bathgate's working past. A map of the area dated 1764 shows Bathgate surrounded by over twenty small farms. Mostly of 100-150 acres, they were mainly owned by large local estates including Balbardie, Boghall, Boghead and Hopetoun and were generally worked by tenant farmers and their families.

From the farm to the plate, Eastman's the butchers claimed to offer the best value to Bathgate housewives. The well-filled shop window in this pre-First World War photograph shows many different cuts of beef, pork and lamb with chops only 6d (two and a half pence in new money) per pound. The trays on the sill of the window contain several different types of sausage and mince. Standing in the doorway wearing their stripped aprons are Hames Hamilton, W. Chalmers and a young A. Speedie who grew up to become one of Bathgate's best known butchers.

Another well-known local businessman, pharmacist Francis Stewart who ran his chemists shop at no.38, King Street.

The covered construction line is the only building to survive from the BMC works at Blackburn. After the closure of the plant it was carefully dismantled and re-erected at Bathgate's sports centre, the Peace Park, in Torphichen Road where it now provides the longest covered running track in Great Britain. Amongst the local athletes who train here is Olympic runner Elliot Bunny. The BMC factory was inaugurated on Wednesday 1 June 1960. The £9m works was erected on 244 acres of land purchased from local farmer Richard Russell of Mosside. The first truck was driven off the Bathgate assembly line on Friday 13 October 1961, an inauspicious date whose ill omen proved only too true. The first tractors produced at Bathgate as part of the David Brown range were showcased at Earls Court in London in December of that year and the six models were also displayed locally at Inch Agricultural Engineers in Blackburn Road with the cheapest priced at only £627. By coincidence the factory also suffered its first strike that same month. It was an unofficial dispute involving only twenty-five of the plant's 5,000-strong labour force, but was symptomatic of the troubles to come. At its height, however, BMC provided work for almost 6,000 people most of whom came in to stay in the area and greatly boosted the population of Bathgate and its surrounding district.

Torphichen Primary School pupils, Michael Laing and Robin Brownlee with their headmaster Bill Hendrie (the author), examine a cutaway display version of one of the 1.5 litre tractor engines manufactured at BMC.

Lines of tractors standing in front of the BMC plant at Blackburn while awaiting export. Demand was never as great as expected and the huge factory eventually closed. The beginning of the end came for the Bathgate factory when world recession in the late 1970s brought job cuts in 1980. Two years later tractor production ceased and although the union shop stewards committee under the leadership of John Swan campaigned hard to find new work, British Leyland, as it was by then known, finally closed in 1986.

TCC and its successor Plessey pioneered the electronics industry in the Bathgate area and laid the foundations for West Lothian's growth to become Scotland's 'Silicon Glen'. Sadly for the town, Motorola, whose premises are pictured, closed in 2001.

Quintiles on the outskirts of Bathgate is now one of the most modern factories in West Lothian.

Another modern building on the outskirts of Bathgate is the town's fire station, opened in 1992 at Starlaw junction. Bathgate's first fire station was opened in Hopetoun Street in 1896 and manned by volunteers who were paid one shilling for every drill which they attended, two shillings for turning out for an actual blaze and a further shilling for every additional hour which they took to extinguish it. The burgh, however, did not acquire a fire engine until 1933 when the Town Council at last agreed to hire a trailer from well-known local iron mongers D.R. Gordon in whose garage behind their shop in Hopetoun Street it was kept. Later that decade the council bought separate premises for a fire station in Muir Road. According to the commemorative booklet published to mark the opening of the present fire station, the pre-war one was lit with gas lamps, but as the Town Council would only allow the expense of buying three gas mantles each month the firemen were often left fumbling in the dark.

Bathgate's own Leerie, the lamp lighter, is seen here atop his ladder carefully lighting one of the fragile little mantles. In those days the town's gas lamps had to be lit by hand each evening at dusk just as Robert Louis Stevenson describes in his well-loved poem in *A Child's Garden of Verses*.

James Gardener and Robert White were two of the hairdressers who provided short back and sides in John Samuel's Barbers Shop. The hand-operated hair clippers, scissors and brush that they used are displayed on the wall behind them. As well as haircuts they were called on daily to provide shaves for Bathgate's businessmen, who preferred the professional touch which the barbers provided with their open cut-throat razors. The cut-throats were sharpened daily using the thick leather razor straps with which the barbers shop was also provided. These were long lengths of hide, similar in length and breadth to the leather tawse with which local teachers doled out punishment to their pupils. Unlike the school straps, which were divided into thongs called tawse tails to increase the sting that they inflicted, they were solid along their entire length. Many Bathgate fathers did however also have razor strops in their bathrooms at home. Officially to hone their own cut-throats, they were on occasion also pressed into service to chastise, or at least threaten, their erring offspring. This perhaps appropriately leads on to the next chapter about Bathgate school days!

Six

Bathgate at School

The first written mention of schooling in Bathgate appears to occur in 1630 when during a Presbyterial visitation it was recorded that John Binnie, 'was the reader, schoolmaster and beadle' of the parish. The beadle was the church officer. The mention of this post, which the teacher also held, and the fact that this earliest mention of education in the town occurred during a visit by the Presbytery elders of the kirk are apt reminders of how closely church and school were linked in earlier times. The high standard of education from which Scottish bairns benefited owed much to the insistence of sixteenth century religious leader John Knox that there should be a school in every parish. On their visit to the Bathgate school, however, the elders were not happy that dominie Binnie was also working as the church officer. They considered these duties were taking up too much of his time and distracting him from his professional work in the classroom and ordered him to give up the post. They did though allow him to remain as the reader in the church, probably because he was one of the few well-educated men in town at the time capable of reading the lessons. He also no doubt needed the extra income as the dominie's salary was very low. The paucity of the dominie's pay was discussed during a later visitation to the school in 1640. It was noted then that many of the local ratepayers, who were referred to as heritors, had not paid their share as laid down by the Scottish Parliament meeting in Edinburgh in 1633. Whether because of his dissatisfaction with his pay or for other reasons Mr Binnie resigned in 1643.

Mr William Forest was appointed as his successor. For the first time there is mention of providing the new dominie with a schoolhouse that was to have a yard in which he could grow vegetables to help eke out his salary, which was to be made up of one merk for every child in the burgh. William Forest taught at the Bathgate school for six years and when he left in 1649 was succeeded by another Mr Forest. Mr Robert Forest proved to be a much more controversial figure. He caused arguments in the town when he promptly forced the closure of what was described as an 'adventure school', a private establishment which was depriving him of some of the income to which he was entitled as parish dominie. The second Mr Forest also caused disputes about his teaching methods, being twice ordered to appear before the Kirk Session to be rebuked about his conduct in the classroom. Whether this was because he was too strict in strapping his scholars or because he was too soft in imposing discipline is not recorded. It is not known how long he remained as dominie because the next appointment noted does not occur until 1673 when Andrew Ross took up the post. By this time the number of pupils was apparently growing because in 1678 an assistant teacher known as 'the doctor' was appointed for the first time..

Best known and most successful of the early Bathgate dominies was Andrew Lyall. He took charge of the parish school in 1696 and taught for twenty years without one single complaint being recorded against him; the Kirk Session recorded that they were "weel pleasit" with his service to the parish. He was succeeded in 1716 by Andrew Simm, after his promotion from Slammanan near Falkirk where he had already been a successful schoolmaster. He was the first Bathgate dominie appointed since the Education Act of 1696, which had been passed just after his predecessor took up post. He was therefore the first schoolmaster selected solely by the ratepayers although they still referred him to the kirk elders for approval of his 'qualifications and guid carriage'.

Throughout the remainder of the eighteenth century and the early years of the following one, education in the town continued to be provided in a succession of small one and two roomed school premises. Yet all that changed dramatically in 1833 with the opening of Bathgate Academy, a picture of whose neoclassical facade and the interesting story of how it came to be constructed appropriately start this section of the book.

This early picture depicts the town's finest building, the Grecian-style Bathgate Academy which was gifted to the burgh by its greatest benefactor John Newland. When this exiled Bathgate bairn died in 1799 in Jamaica, where he had made his fortune as a plantation owner, he left his entire estate 'to erect a free school in the parish of Bathgate.' When details of his will reached Scotland, however, his relatives were disappointed that they were not to receive any of his wealth and so decided to fight for what they considered their rights in the courts. Fortunately for Bathgate, its first Provost Alexander Marjoribanks proved able and willing to contest the case in the Court of Session in Edinburgh. However, despite his best efforts during fifteen years of legal wrangling, the decision reached was that Bathgate should receive only one fifth of the money, which amounted to £14,500. Undeterred, Marjoribanks invested the money wisely until the interest that it accrued provided a sufficient sum in 1831 to start work on the erection of the Academy 'on an open site to the south of the town.' Appropriately the street on which it arose was called Marjoribanks Street, after the man without whose determined efforts it might never have been built.

Bathgate Academy opened in 1833 with a roll of 400 boys and girls with James Fairbairn as its first Rector. As he had only three assistant masters to teach all of these pupils, it is perhaps hardly surprising that the governors were particularly concerned about discipline. They decided that in addition to the corporal punishment that was traditionally used in the town's schools, pupils would be subject to a series of fines. These would range from a half penny for misbehaving on the stairs, which were a great novelty as no previous Bathgate school had possessed a second storey, to two pence if any child dared climb out onto the balustraded roof. This picture taken in 1974 shows pupils of Balbardie Primary after the buildings became an annex of their school.

Boys and girls of an earlier generation seated on long wooden benches in the tiered assembly hall at Bathgate Academy. The school had still not adopted its red and black uniform. The boys wear suits and most of the girls white blouses and navy blue or other dark coloured skirts and black stockings. The girl on the right however is wearing a gym tunic, which became an accepted part of the uniform.

Before the pupils at Bathgate Academy acquired a uniform, the school's well-known janitor, Billy Spokes, wore his with pride, standing on the steps before the entrance on this Newlands Day morning shortly after the end of the First World War. Mr Spokes had served in the forces during that conflict and brought to the Academy an air of discipline which if challenged he never hesitated to enforce with the aid of the short stiff bamboo swagger cane that he carried as his badge of office. As well as being the janitor, in these years long before the General Teaching Council insisted on teaching qualifications, Mr Spokes was also entrusted with instructing the pupils in Physical Training. In summer the somewhat steeply sloping front playground was his parade ground where he drilled the boys and girls, while in winter he put them through their paces each week in the school assembly hall. The fact that the pupils insisted that P.T. on their timetables stood for Physical Torture well sums up the style of his lessons. The gentleman glimpsed on the steps behind the janny was Mr Brown, the Rector of the Academy.

The Academy was badly damaged by fire in 1906 when a blaze swept through the north wing of the school. The disastrous fire started in one of the science laboratories and at its height the whole of the roof caved in. This dramatic view of the shell which remained was taken when pupils turned up for classes the following morning to discover that they had an unexpected days holiday. Their freedom from lessons did not last long however because the Rector and teachers quickly reorganised classes until the damaged wing could be repaired.

On that memorable morning in 1906 the pupils were particularly fascinated to see the new petrol-driven fire engine which had been summoned all the way from Edinburgh to try to fight the spectacular blaze. Unfortunately, the twenty-mile journey took too long for it to be able to help save the north wing of the school. This photograph of the six brass-helmeted, navy-uniformed firemen who made up its crew was taken further along Marjoribanks Street, in front of where the West Lothian College and the Telephone Exchange now stand.

This Bathgate laddie walking along Mid Street was probably a pupil at the Wee Public, whose covered sheds lining the wall of the playground can be seen in the background. The stone, slate-roofed sheds with one side open to the elements provided some shelter for the Wee Public pupils, as they waited for the nine o'clock bell to ring to signal the start of classes. It also sheltered them during playtime, and the lunch hour. when pupils who lived far from home huddled together consuming their pieces, long before the introduction of school meals. On the day of this picture however the weather was fine and dry. The schoolboy was in no hurry to reach home but lingered happily as he whipped his little wooden spinning top, or 'peeries' as he would probably have called it, while two girls cawed their rope and skipped in the background in the trafficless street. This picture gives an unusually detailed glimpse of children's wear of the period with the boy's school cap, his collarless shirt buttoned high up to the neck, his serge jacket and knee breeches worn with home-knitted knee stockings and his tackitty boots. He carried his school books and pencil case in a leather satchel with a shoulder strap, rather than in a school bag worn on his back as became the fashion in later years.

These Bathgate schoolgirls also carried their school books in leather satchels by their sides as they walked home from through the Steel Yard with the Scottish baronial-style post office in the background.

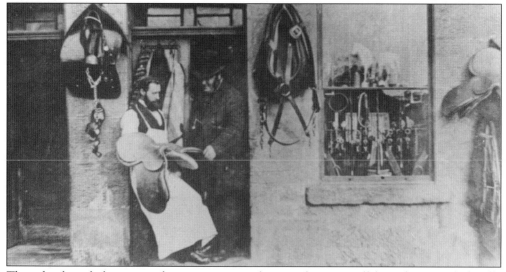

The school satchels seen in the previous two photographs may well have been made locally because Bathgate had its own well-known saddler, Mr William Brownlee in nearby Engine Street. Here he is seen showing a newly completed hand-stitched saddle to the proprietor of the Royal Hotel in the Steel Yard, Sandy Stewart. Mr Stewart was a very good customer. The reason was that as well as running the hotel, he also owned the busy livery yard situated behind the hotel, which was entered through a pend opposite the saddlers where Greig's bakery is now situated. The horses stabled there required many saddles and horse collars like those displayed on either side of the shop doorway. The heavy leather horse collars had to be made individually by Mr Brownlee as every beast varied slightly in shape. As well as being a saddler, Mr Brownlee was an expert on horses. His family had farmed for many years in the Bathgate area before giving up the land to open a dairy in Livery Street, where the yard of the Bennie Museum is now situated. The saddlery was subsequently opened by Mr Brownlee's father in 1858 and went on to trade in the town for almost 130 years, becoming the town's oldest business.

As well as producing articles of saddlery, Brownlee's was known throughout the country as one of Scotland's two top manufacturers of school punishment straps. Their supple effectiveness in administering corporal chastisement was advertised in teachers' magazines, such as the *Education Journal of the Educational Institute of Scotland,* until the late 1970s. The Bathgate belts which Brownlees supplied were only rivalled by the famous or infamous 'Lochgelly Specials' which John Dick crafted in his workshop in the Fife mining village. In this photograph taken in 1974 Mr Stewart Brownlee, great grandson of the founder of the Bathgate business, is seen carefully cutting the thongs of a tawse. The belts made by Brownlees were available in two different lengths and several weights of leather depending on whether they were to be used in primary or secondary schools. Corporal punishment was abolished by Lothian Education Authority on 1 April 1981, with local opinion divided on the wisdom of sparing the strap. A Bathgate-made Brownlee belt is now preserved as an exhibit in the Bennie Museum.

The Lindsay High School and its nearly identical twin St Mary's Academy were opened on adjacent sites in September 1931. The completion of these two large school buildings and a third similarly designed building in Bo'ness completely revolutionised education in West Lothian. In Bathgate the opening of the two new schools resulted in the introduction of the tripartite system of secondary schooling with the Academy specialising in academic courses, the Lindsay High providing technical and commercial subjects and Bathgate Junior Secondary offering practical courses. St Mary's Academy fitted into this pattern by providing what were described as senior secondary courses for Roman Catholic children from all parts of the county and multilateral classes for all Catholics from the Bathgate area. As one of Scotland's few technical high schools, the Lindsay possessed excellently equipped science laboratories, technical workshops and commercial and domestic science classrooms. It even had its own underground mine beneath the school, in which boys could receive specialist training for work in the local coal and shale industries. The Lindsay High School was named after the Rev. John Lindsay, minister of St John's Church and chairman of West Lothian Education Committee when it opened in 1931. It closed at the end of June 1967 when a further change in educational thinking led to its merger with the other non-denominational secondary schools in the town into one comprehensive school at Boghall.

The school captains and prefects of the Lindsay High School pictured in 1964.

Girls from Bathgate Junior Secondary School, whose building is now occupied by Balbardie Primary School, photographed in their gym uniforms during the early years of the twentieth century. The girls are all pictured wearing plimsolls. These shoes worn for physical education classes had different names in various parts of Scotland. In Glasgow and the West they were usually known as 'sannies' derived from 'sand shoes' because they were often bought for playing on the sands when city families went 'doon the watter for the Fair'. In Bathgate they were generally referred to as 'gutties' because the soles were made from guttaperca or 'rubbers' because of the flexible nature of the soles.

The style of sports outfit and the amount of freedom which girls were allowed to enjoy had changed radically by the time of this photograph, taken half a century later. The prize-winning Lindsay High School netball team proudly displayed the trophy that they had won as West Lothian Schools Under-15 League Winners in 1965. The girls in their crisp white gym blouses and chocolate brown gym pants, which were part of the Lindsay High's strictly enforced brown and gold uniform, are from left to right: Teresa Fairley, Jean Wilko, Fay Watson, Anne Cunningham, Barbara McIntyre, Christine Fraser and Ann Edwards.

That same year the girls of the Lindsay High School's Under-13 netball team also won the West Lothian Schools Championship for their age group. Pictured with the gymnasium of the new Bathgate Academy, which the Lindsay had occupied for a year on its own before the merger of the Bathgate secondary schools, the girls of the winning team are from left to right: Carol Kerr, Margaret Steel, Anna McDonald, Elizabeth Steel, Morag Ferguson and Morag Kelly, with Helen Riddell and Marie Campbell kneeling in front. The girls were trained by the Lindsay High School's hard working physical education teacher, Helen Inglis, whose father Jack was West Lothian Education Authority's well-known pioneering outdoor education adviser. Helen married her colleague in the P.E. department Peter Reid. Their daughter Heather has won nationwide fame and popularity as the weather forecaster on BBC Television's flagship news programme *Reporting Scotland*.

Helen Inglis at work in the gymnasium at the new Bathgate Academy. She is supervising young gymnast Marion Williams who is performing a handstand on the box while her third year classmates Elizabeth Steel, Jessie Turner and Carol Currie balance on the beams.

Another of the Lindsay High School's shield-winning netball teams was made up by the senior girls who are seen here posing proudly for the photographer on the front steps of the new Academy building at Boghall in 1967.

Seated on the front steps at the Lindsay High School are the boys of the school football team, who were always looked upon as formidable rivals by other teams in the West Lothian Schools' League.

Another strong eleven from the Lindsay High.

The Lindsay High School maintained its sporting prowess right up until its final year of existence which its pupils spent occupying the new Academy building, where this cup-winning football team was pictured. The boys who made up this Under-13 team were, back row, from left to right: Deacon, Young, Smith, McLaughlan, Logan and Mairs; front row: Menzies, Liddell, Hamilton, Millar, Borrowman and Thomson. Boys at the Lindsay High were always addressed by their surnames, a rather archaic practice that continued until the end of the school's thirty-six years in existence.

Rector James Brodlie and his staff posed for a final staff photograph beside the front steps of the old school before moving to the new Academy building at Boghall where Mr Brodlie was appointed headmaster of the combined Bathgate non demoninational secondary schools. He is flanked in this photograph on the right by Deputy Rector Mr Brash and on the left by Lady Adviser Miss Helen Cox who was subsequently succeeded in this important role by modern languages specialist Miss Jessie Heigh, seated next to Mr Brash. Lindsay High former pupils will also easily pick out other well-known teachers including seated in the front row, principal English teacher, Dr Andrew Bain, and heads of geography, history, commercial and technical subjects Willie Auld, Sandy Niven, Jimmy Wardrope and Neil Sturgeon.

Rector James Brodlie, Deputy Rector Mr Brash and Lady Adviser Miss Cox also posed on the steps of the Lindsay High for this photograph of the school captains Catherine Lambie and Alan Sturgeon and 1965 sixth formers including John Aitkman, George Merry, Gordon Rhind, Chalmers twins Keith and Kenneth, Stefan Mackolecki, Jeffrey Jennings, Angus Cowe, John Mair, Sandy Waddell, George Ritchie, Iain Storrie, William Collie, Keneth Mackenzie and James Currie.

This photograph of an outdoor art lesson taken in 1974 also shows off the new premises of Bathgate Academy on a hillside to the east of the town at Boghall.

The War Memorial Clock originally situated above the main entrance of the Lindsay High School has been moved to a similar setting at Bathgate Academy at Boghall. This photograph, taken in September 2000, shows prefect Laura-Jane Riach chatting during a morning interval to her friend Kim Mann who is a member of the school's Student Council.

St Mary's Academy was situated on an adjacent site to the east of the Lindsay High School. Although their playgrounds adjoined each other, there was seldom any trouble between the pupils of the two schools. Their combined rivalry was rather reserved to taking on the boys and girls of Bathgate Academy who on winter mornings had to dodge a hail of snowballs as they made their way along to their school in Marjoribanks Street. This rivalry extended to the sports field where the St Mary's pupils proudly wore their royal blue and gold colours. After 1967, St Mary's also occupied the former premises of the Lindsay High until it was itself closed and its pupils transferred to St Kentigern's High School, Blackburn as a result of the restructuring of denominational education in West Lothian. This included the closure of Our Lady's Secondary, Broxburn and the opening of the new St Margaret's Academy in Livingston. Like Bathgate Academy, St Mary's was famed for its end of summer term productions of the Gilbert and Sullivan operettas. The school's long-serving Principal Teacher of Art, Johnnie Doherty, loved to recall how during the final performance of the Mikado he slipped on stage and dressed as a coolie mingled with the fifth and sixth year boys in the chorus while puffing away at a pipe. Its smoke was spotted by the school's well-known ice hockey playing Rector Dr McCabe, who intended strapping the culprit in his study the next morning, only to discover that it was his senior art master! Such tricks made him a popular figure with the generations of St Mary's pupils whom he taught during his fifty years on the staff of the school.

Houses have now been built on the sites of both the Lindsay High School and St Mary's Academy, but the names of the two schools will be preserved as the estate has been named Lindsay Gardens. It is promised that one of its streets will be named St Mary's Avenue.

The New Public School was opened in Torphichen Street in 1904. It later became known as Bathgate Junior Secondary School and since 1968 the building has been occupied by Balbardie Primary School.

With thick stone walls and a slate roof, Balbardie Primary still maintains the look of a very traditionally Scottish school. Yet under the headships of the late David Cook, who went on to become West Lothian's senior educational adviser, and his successor Mrs Myra MacPherson the school has developed a nationally recognised reputation for its modern teaching methods. This fact was recognised by the award of an MBE to Mrs MacPherson for her services to Scottish Education during the twenty years that she has been in charge. Although the front of the school building looks little changed since it opened in 1904, the interior has been modernised and a new block of classrooms erected to the north of the original premises.

As early as the 1920s, the Torphichen Street School was adopting progressive teaching techniques, introducing its young pupils to the enjoyment of drama through this production of 'Simple Simon and the Pieman'. It is interesting to note that under their white apron costumes, all of the boys wore school shorts with knee-high knitted stockings folded over at the top and kept up with tight fitting elastic garters.

Nowadays the Balbardie pupils are still proud of their maroon and gold uniform but it is more comfortable, in the form of cotton sweatshirts for both boys and girls. This playground scene also shows the school's garden, where much project work is carried out. The stone built cottages in the background in Torphichen Street are as old as the school building. Those on the left are unaltered from the time they were erected a century ago, but those on the right have had their accommodation expanded by the creation of first floor bedrooms by utilising the space under the pitched slate roof.

Balbardie Primary School has worked hard to establish excellent relationships with not only parents but also grandparents, as seen during this open day whose fine weather made it possible for afternoon teas to be served outdoors in the playground.

Classes at Balbardie primary also often make use of the playground for open-air lessons.

For many years Balbardie Primary has been famed for the magnificent decorated tableau which staff, janitors, friends of the school and pupils have worked hard to create as a highlight of Newland's Day processions. This one took as its colourful theme 'Snow White and The Seven Dwarves' and after its successful appearance on Bathgate's Procession day went on, like its predecessors, to win many awards at events such as Linlithgow Marches, Bo'ness Children's Fair Festival and Whitburn and Armadale gala days.

Balbardie Primary was chosen for the launch of West Lothian Council's anti litter campaign, 'Bung It In The Bin', and the pupils were thrilled to enjoy a visit from a real 'live' Womble.

Wearing his gold chain of office, Provost of West Lothian, Councillor Joe Thomas looked on proudly with his deputy, Councillor Allister Mackie, and other officials as the anti-litter campaign 'Bung It In The Bin' was launched in the assembly hall at Balbardie Primary. It was also introduced at all other primary schools in the county. This photograph shows the Balbardie pupils neatly turned out in their modern school uniform of maroon coloured cotton sweatshirts. Some of the girls still wear traditional white school blouses and ties but most pupils choose gold soft-collared cotton polo shirts; it is interesting to note that even the smallest boys now wear long grey trousers and the girls black tights with their grey school skirts.

The modern buildings of Boghall Primary School were erected in 1958 to cater for the boys and girls of the adjoining housing scheme set on the hillside to the east of the town. This picture was taken in 1973.

Boghall Primary was officially opened inn October 1958 and to mark the occasion all of the staff and pupils assembled in the playground for this photo.

This class photograph was taken at Boghall Primary in 1966. The boys in the front row are seated on coconut mats borrowed from the school gym, while the girls in the second row filled two of the long benches also borrowed from the gym.

Two years later on the school's twentieth anniversary, teacher Mr Cowan posed with his class for this souvenir picture. The headmaster at the time was Mr Edward Millar. The school's present head is Mrs Alison Fox.

St Mary's Primary is one of two Roman Catholic primary schools providing denominational education in Bathgate. The other is the smaller St Columba's Primary in the Boghall area of the town.

Murrayfield Primary School was built to cope with the influx of population into the Bathgate suburb with the building of the British Motor Corporation Truck and Tractor Works in the 1960s. Its first headmaster was Mr William Howie. He was succeeded in 1972 by the author, and in 1977 Mrs Margaret Mills became the school's first woman headteacher.

Murrayfield Primary School's fine modern assembly hall was the setting for this music practice c.1975.

Teacher Mrs Mary Murphy, who later became head of Our Lady's Primary School, Stoneyburn, reads to her Primary 7 class during the mid 1970s.

Murrayfield Primary School pupils featured in the Scottish Television schools' series *Play Fair* and here they watch intently as one of the shows in which they featured is transmitted. The moral education series dealt with many topics at the time considered controversial for pupils to be encouraged to discuss, from gangs to bullying. It proved so successful and popular with schools throughout Britain, Ireland and the Channel Islands that it became the country's longest running schools' series, being broadcast every year for a decade.

Extra curricular activities were also a popular feature of life for pupils at Murrayfield Primary.

Nature Club was a popular choice of activity at Murrayfield Primary, especially when there was a real live specimen such as this hedgehog to examine.

Chess also was featured at Murrayfield Primary School's weekly school club.

Murrayfield's progressive methods led to much interest not just in Scotland but from abroad and this picture of boys and girls waiting to begin an open-air gym lesson was taken during the visit of a Russian delegation to the school.

Visitors from Lithuania took this photograph of the women members of staff at Murrayfield Primary School during a visit during the mid-1970s. They are pictured in the entrance hall of the school and behind them on the wall can be seen the dedication plaque. The school takes its name from the fact that it stands on the site of one of the fields that belonged to the Murray family who occupied Blackburn House. The school's badge is the yellow broom, the flower of the Murray clan.

These infant pupils posed for a class photograph taken in front of the Murrayfield Primary School's staff room on a spring day during the early 1970s.

As ever, school playtime was popular at Murrayfield Primary.

The dress rehearsal for Murrayfield Primary School's production of *Oliver Twist*. The headmaster and show's director, William F. Hendrie, is giving some last minute tips to the Artful Dodger as he practises picking Fagin's pocket. Looking on is Assistant Headmaster, Mr William Millan, whose colourfully designed scenery and props added much to all of the school's many stage productions.

Seven

Bathgate at Play

For many decades Bathgate has been well provided with a wide range of leisure and sporting facilities. One of the earliest organised sports was curling, with a club formed in 1811. Curling's summer equivalent, bowling, began in the town at the Bathgate Bowling Club situated on land between Academy Street and Mid Street in 1862. Six years later a second club was opened at Grayshall, close to the site now occupied by the Glenmavis Club. The owner of the Bathgate Club's green, Thomas Johnson, unfortunately became bankrupt and its members had therefore to join the rival club in Torphichen Street. Today bowls is still a popular sport in the town, with in addition to the Torphichen Street club, outdoor lawns at Balbardie Road and in Kirkton Park, where Spring Grove Club plays throughout the spring, summer and autumn months. In winter Balbardie Leisure Stadium in Peace Park provides indoor facilities thus making it a year round sport. Football as an organised sport is first reported in the Courier in 1879 and at one time Bathgate played in the prestigious Scottish League. Golf was first played locally in 1892 and fifteen years later the original nine-hole course was expanded to a full eighteen laid out on Meikle Inch. The indoor swimming pool was opened in Mid Street in 1934. A more modern innovation is the Bathgate Sports Centre whose first facilities opened in 1982. While sports and leisure activities take place all year in Bathgate there are two specific highlights each summer, the Highland Games on the last Saturday in May and John Newlands Procession Day one week later on the first Saturday in June. The Highland Games began as a pipe band contest in 1974 and are now well established as an important event in the Scottish Highland Games circuit. Procession Day dates back much further to 1844.

The building of highly ornate decorated arches has always been a feature of Bathgate's Newlands Procession Day celebrations. This magnificent example of the arch builders' craft was erected at Drumcross Road during the early 1900s. Like most Bathgate arches it was built on a large timber frame and covered with clipped green box wood gathered from the grounds of Balbardie House and other neighbouring large estates as far away as Wallhouse at Torphichen. It was finally finished with flowers and other decorations made from brightly coloured crepe paper.

This second arch was built around the same period to celebrate a Procession Day. It spanned Whitburn Road and was photographed looking through it towards the buildings on the far side of the Steel Yard, as George Place was still then called. It was surmounted by a large crown and a lion and the two smaller arches which spanned the pavements on either side of the street were topped with white Prince of Wales' feathers. As in the previous picture, the pride of the people who lived nearby is obvious as they turned out to be photographed framed by their masterpiece.

The photographer appears to have arrived unannounced to photograph this broad arch as only the man on the corner appears to be taking any notice of him at work. The arch was erected at the foot of North Bridge Street where it joins South Bridge Street. Apart from the absence of a crowd of people the other noteworthy fact is the equal absence of traffic. It was these quieter street conditions which made it possible to build such large arches over main streets in the town. Nowadays the position of any modern arch has to be given careful consideration in order to avoid interrupting traffic.

The crowds are back out in force in this photograph taken of an arch in Livery Street looking east. Beyond it is an intriguing glimpse of Bathgate's original picture house, the Cinema House.

The old Cinema House is seen again in the background in this second picture of Livery Street, with the Roman Catholic Church in the right foreground.

On the evening of Procession Day, however, Bathgate bairns were perhaps more likely to seek their entertainment at the travelling funfair which only visited the town for a short period at this time of year. On the occasion that this photograph was taken one of the big attractions at the shows was a very early white-knuckle ride. It appears to have been a version of the modern 'Jungle Ride' with fully rigged Viking sailing boats bobbing up and down on an undulating circular track. It is interesting to note that a similar ride on a Scandinavian theme, with Viking sailing ships, is still a popular attraction at Copenhagen's famous Tivoli Fairground. On the gable wall in the background can be seen a large advertisement for the town's well-known Roberts's Livery Stables, rivals of the livery yard at the Royal Hotel in the Steel Yard. It offers open carriages, small brakes and mounting coaches for hire. No doubt most of the carriages and brakes would have been in great demand earlier in the day by participants who wished to ride the streets of the town in the Newland's Procession parade.

Opposite:
Originally thought to be a rare view of the shows on a visit to neighbouring Whitburn, this early Edwardian photograph is now known to be of the gallopers on a roundabout in Bathgate on a Newland's Procession Day. This early steam driven roundabout bears the slogan *Grand Continental* on its canopy, but it is definitely of British construction. This can be told from the fact that at fairs in Scotland the intricately carved, beautifully painted horses with their gilded manes always turned in a clockwise direction as seen here. Thus their riders could mount these wooden steeds from the correct side, a tradition maintained to the present day. This beautifully composed shot shows a little boy in his cap and jacket with its Eton collar and a little girl in her felt hat, long jacket shirt and black stockings. They approach the roundabout with a sense of anticipation of the excitement to come on this yearly outing to the shows.

This appearance in the town of this dancing bear also drew crowds to watch its antics as it performed in the Steel Yard in front of the Royal Hotel. Bears such as this were often brought to Scottish towns during the years prior to the outbreak of the First World War by Hungarian gypsies, who caught and taught them to perform tricks. In those days, before people were so sensitive to animal rights, they could earn money from such street performances.

Another visitor to Bathgate which would prove equally controversial nowadays was the hunt. The members of the Linlithgowshire and Stirlingshire Hunt are seen riding up Engine Street in top hats and pink coats, pursued by a group of excited small boys. One of the boys is bare footed. Although still legal in Scotland, fox hunting no longer takes place in West Lothian. Not only is there a ban on hunting over council owned land in the Bathgate Hills and elsewhere, but the building of the M8 and M9 which carve their way across the district has made it difficult to give the hounds a good safe run. This picture must have been taken after 1908, as the spires of the Roman Catholic Church of the Immaculate Conception which are seen in the background were completed in that year.

The Procession was a dreich affair on this soaking wet Newlands Day in 1909 but umbrella-carrying crowds still doggedly lined Engine Street to watch the horse-drawn carriages and bands pass by. Despite the weather, Livingston-based photographer Robert Braid took this picture and sold it as a postcard view of the day when the Procession was nearly washed out. He took his picture from the junction of Engine Street with South Bridge Street and Hopetoun Street.

The sun shone for the Procession Day for which these shop premises at the foot of Hopetoun Street, and the Provost's lamp which stood on the pavement in front of them, were colourfully decorated. The lamp was erected there for the ceremonial reason of denoting the home of Provost Robertson and for the practical one of lighting the way for visitors who wished to consult him. Provost Robertson was the proprietor of the ironmonger's store on the left of the picture. In the centre, the barber's red and white pole with its gold knob on the end marks the premises of McGill the hairdresser and from the display in its window the shop on the right must be a family draper's business.

Another popular place on Procession Night would undoubtedly have been the Dreadnought Hotel in Whitburn Road. It opened in 1901 and takes its name not from the First World War battleships, which it pre-dates, but from the war cry of the clan MacDuff. Its owner was Scott Gibson who had previously been the tenant of the town's Commercial Hotel. Mr Gibson's name was painted on the gable of the new hotel for every passer-by to observe. He died in 1916 but his widow continued to manage the busy hotel until 1923 when she left the town and their son emigrated to the United States. The Scottish baronial-style frontage of the Dreadnought still presents a most impressive facade on Whitburn Road. Here it is pictured in September 1999 after extensive renovations made it one of the most modern and comfortable hotels in West Lothian. In addition to its bars the Dreadnought has an excellent restaurant which caters both for many guests and for non-residents. At the rear the hotel also possesses its own nightclub where discos are held regularly at weekends. It is now owned by Ian Murtage and managed by his wife Marilyn, a former Lindsay High School pupil.

On Wednesdays and at weekends an open-air market now makes Whitburn Road one of the busiest places in town.

Stall holders travel from all over Central Scotland to trade at Bathgate Market, held three days a week in Whitburn Road.

Customers also come from many other parts of West Lothian seeking bargains at Bathgate market.

Saturday shoppers enjoy a seat in the gardens in South Bridge Street. West Lothian Council's St David's House with its coat of arms can also be seen.

The Glenmavis is one of the oldest pubs in Bathgate. Situated in Gideon Street, the earliest reference to it under this name occurred around 1850 but there is known to have been a tavern in this area long before then and the Glenmavis is probably a continuation of the same business if not the same building.

The Kaim Park became a hotel in 1948. Earlier in the century, as a private house belonging to Mr Enoch Glen, who made his money in the shale oil business, its stables, which are now occupied by one of the hotel's bars, were home to his collection of prize-winning trotting ponies. The most famous was Torchfire, who became a world champion. When Torchfire died in 1921 he was buried in the grounds of Kaim Park; the famous stallion is still remembered by the hotel's function suite, which bears his name.

Bathgate's newest hotel is the Express by Holiday Inn, conveniently situated at Starlaw Junction just off the M8 motorway. The modern seventy-four bedroom hotel is operated as part of a nationwide chain by the brewers Bass who also own the adjacent Bathgate Farm Inn, which is part of the Brewers Fayre chain and offers family dining facilities. This new development was opened in 1997.

Driving into town from Starlaw roundabout the road now passes these new homes at Lindsay Gardens on the site of the former Lindsay High School and St Mary's Academy.

Further intro town on this same route an attractive stone gateway leads into the town's Kirkton Park. The park was officially opened in June 1927 by the Secretary of State for Scotland, the Rt Hon. Sir John Gilmour, who performed the ceremony on a wet Saturday.

Public Park, Bathgate

This splendid view of Kirkton Park shows the Pavilion, which cost £7,533 to build, and the bowling green and four tennis courts, as seen from a vantage point above Puir Wife's Brae. It was taken in the late 1920s or early 1930s and sold as a popular picture postcard view.

The model yachting and paddling pond was a popular feature of Kirkton Park in earlier decades, as was the shell-shaped bandstand. This cost just over £700 to erect, not including the 500 folding chairs provided to seat the large audiences who used to come regularly to enjoy the concerts staged there throughout the summer season. A proposed tea room was never built, but a putting green was later opened on the hillside above the tennis courts.

The road then continues towards the heart of the town at George Square, passing the new railway station in King Street. This old view shows a happy group about to depart on a summer outing from the town's original Upper Station with its wrought-iron footbridge leading over to the opposite platform. It gives a wonderfully detailed picture of the fashions of the period and especially of the variety of headwear from the men's flat caps to their straw boaters and the ladies' elaborate bonnets.

The Upper Station with passengers waiting on the platform for the train.

Around this same period in the early 1920s, charabanc outings were an exciting novelty. Here a party of adults and children, possibly members of the congregation of Bathgate High Church, are seen setting out for the day in an open top charabanc with a West Lothian SX registration plate. They are crowded together on its long bench seats, the doorways to which are guarded with little wooden fence doors. Along the sides are wooden running boards similar to those found on train passenger carriages. Under the mud wings, the tyres appear to be of solid rubber. Notice also the small carbine-lit headlights.

This group of adults and children enjoyed the luxury of a covered charabanc when they set off on their outing. They may have been members of the High Church on a Sunday school picnic. Notice again the familiar West Lothian registration letters SX on the number-plate.

Another charabanc outing was a highlight of the 1910 summer for these workers. They were employed on the building of Greig's Emporium, the town's department store which formerly dominated the scene on the corner of Whitburn Road opposite the Steel Yard. A piano accordionist to provide entertainment is seated playing in the centre of the group.

These Bathgate laddies were caught and snapped by well-known Livingston photographer and publisher of picture postcards, Robert Braid, as they enjoyed a swim in the Mill Pond while some of their friends picnicked.

The Bennie Museum possesses one of the best local history collections in Scotland and is the ideal place to visit to find out more about Bathgate's past. Its name comes from the Bennie family who originally owned these cottages and gifted them to the town for this purpose. The extensive work of converting the property was led by local art teacher Willie Millan, who served first on the staff of the Lindsay High School and was later appointed Assistant Headmaster of Murrayfield Primary, Blackburn. Mr Millan is now the voluntary curator of the little museum his efforts have created and whose wonderfully esoteric collection owes much to his inquiring nature. The Bennie Museum first opened to the public in May 1989 before being officially opened in May 1990 by Mrs. Kathleen Dalyell, wife of local MP Tam Dalyell. Both husband and wife had supported the project from the outset. The museum now also has a life-size model of a washhouse set up in the old stables where the Bennies, who were contractor hauliers, kept their horses before acquiring their first lorry. The hand-operated petrol pump which they set up to fuel their earlier motor vehicles was amongst the original objects salvaged by Willie Millan and is now on display in the museum. The museum provides a pleasant setting on a summer's day for visitors to stroll back in time and recall Bathgate's past, with the help of many exhibits. These range from school uniforms and the big wooden counter from John Hardy's drapers shop over which they were sold, to examples of articles made in the Bathgate Glass Works and a large number of souvenirs of past Newlands Days.

What better way to bring this look at Bathgate's past to a close than the invitation to 'stop me and buy one', issued by this ice cream vendor as he pushed his barrow along Mid Street shortly before the outbreak of the First World War. Was he perhaps a member of one of Bathgate's Italian immigrant families, the Bonis, the Crollas or the Serafinis, who chose to make their home here? Their delicious ice cream cones and wafers delighted not only the young lad and the two beautifully dressed little girls with their straw bonnets who appear in this picture, but also generation upon generation of Bathgate bairns down through the decades.